PROGRAM EVALUATION *for* SPORTDIRECTORS

James L. Kestner
American Sport Education Program

Human Kinetics

Library of Congress Cataloging-in-Publication Data

Kestner, James L., 1964-
    Program evaluation for sportdirectors / James L. Kestner.
        p. cm.
    ISBN 0-88011-505-X
    1. Sports administration--Evaluation.   2. Athletic directors-
-Rating of.   I. Title.   II. Title: Program evaluation for sport
directors
    GV713.K47   1996
    796'.06'9--dc20
                                           95-24267
                                              CIP

ISBN: 0-88011-505-X

Form 3.1 adapted with permission from the following sources: *Youth SportDirector Guide* (pp. 4.25–4.28), by R. Martens, 1995, Champaign, IL: Human Kinetics. Copyright 1995 by Rainer Martens. • *American Coaching Effectiveness Program Level 2 Sport Law Workbook* (pp. 40–41), by American Coaching Effectiveness Program, 1985, Champaign, IL: Human Kinetics. Copyright 1985 by Human Kinetics Publishers, Inc. • "Safety Checklists: Making Indoor Areas Hazard-Free," by J.R. Olson, 1985, *Athletic Business*, 9(11), pp. 36–38. Copyright 1985 by Athletic Business Magazine.

Form 3.2 is from *Youth SportDirector Guide* (pp. 4.29–4.32, respectively) by Rainer Martens. Copyright 1995 by Rainer Martens. Reprinted with permission.

Developmental Editor: Jan Colarusso Seeley; **Assistant Editors:** Erin Cler and Henry Woolsey; **Editorial Assistant:** Andrew Starr; **Copyeditor:** Cheryl Resetarits; **Proofreader:** Anne M. Byler; **Typesetter and Layout Artist:** Francine Hamerski; **Text and Cover Designer:** Stuart Cartwright; **Author Photo:** Andrea Whitesell; **Illustrators:** Patrick Griffin, cartoons; and Stuart Cartwright; **Printer:** Versa Press

Printed in the United States of America   10 9 8 7 6 5 4 3 2 1

Human Kinetics
P.O. Box 5076, Champaign, IL 61825-5076
1-800-747-4457

Canada: Human Kinetics, Box 24040,
Windsor, ON N8Y 4Y9
1-800-465-7301 (in Canada only)

Europe: Human Kinetics, P.O. Box IW14,
Leeds LS16 6TR, United Kingdom
(44) 1132 781708

Australia: Human Kinetics, 2 Ingrid Street,
Clapham 5062, South Australia
(08) 371 3755

New Zealand: Human Kinetics, P.O. Box 105-231,
Auckland 1
(09) 523 3462

Contents

Series Preface   v

Acknowledgments   vii

PART ONE: A BLUEPRINT FOR SUCCESSFUL EVALUATION   **1**

The Program Evaluation Process   2

PART TWO: PERSONNEL EVALUATION   **11**

Troubles With Checklists   11

Solutions From Educators   12

Tools for Evaluating Athletic Program Personnel   13

Procedures for Conducting Your Personnel Evaluation   14

Guidelines for Effective Use of Personnel Evaluation Tools   23

PART THREE: FACILITY, EQUIPMENT, AND PROGRAM EVALUATION   **33**

Facilities and Equipment   33

Program Offerings   37

FORMS

Form 1.1: Identifying Evaluation Needs   43

Form 2.1: Summative Coach Evaluation Instrument   45

Form 2.2: Colleague Questionnaire   56

Form 2.3: Athlete Questionnaire   67

Form 2.4: Parent Questionnaire   70

Form 2.5: Coach Self-Appraisal Form   73

Form 2.6: Goal Identification Form   76

Form 2.7: Goal-Setting Conference Form 78

Form 2.8: Progress Appraisal Conference Form 80

Form 2.9: Personnel Evaluation Summary Form 83

Form 3.1: Facilities Inspection Checklist 86

Form 3.2: Equipment Inspection Checklist 90

Form 3.3: Record-Keeping Checklist 94

Form 3.4: Facility Analysis Form 95

Form 3.5: Equipment Analysis Form 98

Form 3.6: Facilities and Equipment Questionnaire 101

Form 3.7: Facility and Equipment Evaluation Summary Form 103

Form 3.8: Sport Director's Program Identification Form 105

Form 3.9: Sport Program Questionnaire 108

Form 3.10: Program Analysis Summary Form 110

Appendix American Sport Education Program (ASEP)
  Leader Level Resources 115

About the Author 117

About ASEP 118

Series Preface

The SportDirector Series is a revolutionary approach to the craft of managing athletic programs. Underlying the resources in this series is a set of principles drawn from a careful examination of the day-to-day responsibilities sport directors face. These principles have been framed as a sequence of tests, which each series resource has been designed to pass:

- Is the resource practical?
- Is it affordable?
- Does it save time?
- Is it easy to use?
- Is it up-to-date?
- Is it flexible enough to meet different programs' needs?
- Does using one resource from the series make it easier to use others?

To ensure that every resource passes these tests, we have worked closely with an editorial advisory board of prominent, experienced athletic directors from across the nation. With the board's assistance, we have developed the series to enable you to benefit from the latest thinking in directing sport programs. Each resource leads you carefully through three steps: planning, implementing, and evaluating.

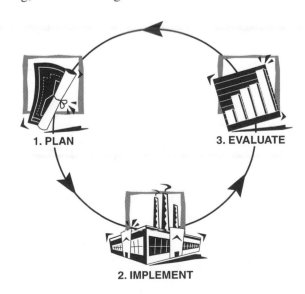

1. PLAN

3. EVALUATE

2. IMPLEMENT

What's so new about the approach? Nothing—until you actually apply it. That's where the series really breaks the mold. Besides telling you how important it is to plan for success in directing your programs, each resource will lead you step-by-step through that planning process. Forms and exercises will help you explore your role and philosophy within the organization, examine your particular needs, and then develop an effective plan of action. In each SportDirector resource these steps are applied specifically to the task at hand. For example, it is essential to assess your needs carefully as you carry out each of your program responsibilities: How you assess promotional needs, however, will differ significantly from how you assess personnel management needs. The series follows the same practical approach to lead you through the implementation and evaluation of your plan.

This approach is possible only because the series authors are experts not only in sport management but also in the specific areas they write about. With the help of the editorial advisory board, these authors translate their knowledge into practical, easy-to-follow recommendations, ready-to-use forms and checklists, and countless practical tips and examples so that you will come away with better ideas for directing your program. The authors also help you take advantage of the latest technology.

New and experienced interscholastic athletic directors alike will find that these resources take into account their widespread responsibilities and limited staff and funding assistance. Directors of Olympic national governing body club sport programs and other national and state sport directors will find valuable tools to enhance their efficiency and increase their effectiveness. Students of sport administration will find these resources valuable companions for understanding how to step into the field with confidence to succeed. And all sport directors will find that these tools help them to help the athletes, coaches, parents, and others in their organizational community.

Even more than a leader, you are the architect of your organization's athletic community. As you design and oversee the construction and maintenance of that community, you are in a unique position to ensure that the program achieves a common purpose. The SportDirector Series is conceived not only to help you attend to your everyday duties but also to coalesce your efforts to carry out your program's mission—to make your athletic community the best it can be.

—Jim Kestner

Seeing the glimmer of the future reflected in the eyes of children,
I dedicate this book to my wife Tami and our son Maxwell.

Acknowledgments

This book culminates my efforts under the guidance of many mentors and with the support of many friends and family members. This expression of my gratitude is small compared with the benefits I have received, but I offer it with sincerity to my mentors, Jim Ward, Tom McGreal, Paul Thurston, Bob Nielsen, Michael Loudon, Vic Bobb, Fred Preston, and Jim Quivey; to my editor, Jan Colarusso Seeley; my assistant in testing these resources, Jessie Daw; and the athletic directors and schools who opened their doors in support of this project, Jim Graham, Liz Osborn, and Urbana and Unity High School coaches, faculty, administrators, athletes, and parents; to my director, Karen Partlow, and ASEP founder, Rainer Martens; and most of all to my parents (all four of you), my family, and my loving wife, Tami.

Part One

A Blueprint for
Successful Evaluation

Every day, your position as sport director requires you to make countless decisions. To make good decisions, you must have a solid understanding of your athletic program. You need to be able to answer questions like these:

- What is the philosophy behind your athletic program?

- What coaching behaviors represent the minimum acceptable competence in your program?

- Can you verify that all of your coaches make safety a priority?

- Do your coaches maintain accurate records?

- Are your facilities safe, adequate, and cost effective for your program offerings?

- Is equipment maintained, distributed, collected, and stored properly?

- Does your program offer equal access to athletes regardless of gender, race and ethnicity, and socioeconomic status?

- Are your program offerings the best use of financial resources?

Until now, few resources have been available to the sport director who sought to answer these questions on a regular, systematic basis. Although a few years of experience provide many directors with ideas about valuable resources, the time necessary to create those resources is often prohibitive.

Program Evaluation for Sport Directors has been developed to meet your needs as an interscholastic athletic director, an education director for an Olympic national governing body, an aspiring sport director, or anyone in between. Part One of this guide delineates the process of preparing for an effective program evaluation. Part Two focuses on personnel evaluation and presents a two-pronged approach to this important evaluation component. Part Three turns to the evaluation of facilities, equipment, and program offerings. In addition to checklists and surveys, this guide assists in organizing and keeping records and provides methods for examining the cost effectiveness of an athletic program.

This book provides important tools for program evaluation. The tools appear as 20 forms that can be photocopied and adapted to specific settings.

THE PROGRAM EVALUATION PROCESS

The approach you take in evaluating your program should be dictated by the needs of both you and your organization. When you face an evaluation, consider your goals, using this guide to select the best tool for the job. The tools in this guide have been designed to work together, but you might find some tools more appropriate for your needs than others. Regardless of the tools used, there are certain steps you can take to ensure that your program evaluation is as valuable as possible.

Six Steps for Effective Program Evaluation

Effective and efficient program evaluation requires careful planning. These six basic steps—which the book helps you follow—will lead you to successful evaluations.

1. Reflect on personal and organizational philosophies.
2. Identify key roles.
3. Assess evaluation needs.
4. Develop an evaluation plan.
5. Implement the evaluation plan.
6. Review and revise the evaluation plan.

As you can see, there's a lot to do before you actually implement your program evaluation plan. By carefully attending to the first 4 steps—the plan-ning stages—you can implement your plan with fewer surprises, and by reviewing and revising your plan, you can improve each year's program evaluation process. Let's get started!

Step 1: Reflect on Personal and Organizational Philosophies

Don't skip this step! Before you can begin to evaluate your program, you need to answer a few important questions. What skills, traits, and knowledge do you value in your head coaches? Assistants? Trainers? Administrative assistants? As you think about the answers to these questions, you may start to ask others. What would you consider a successful year? Why is an athletic program important to you? To your coaches? Your athletes? Their parents? The answers to these questions vary among organizations and even among individuals within a single organization. However, only by answering these questions can you hope to develop an effective program evaluation system. Here's an example of how important this first step can be.

Mike is a new athletic director at East High School. When he visits Coach Rentschler's volleyball practice for his first evaluation, though, Mike can hardly believe his eyes. When one of the players falls into the net after missing a spike attempt, her coach makes the athlete do push-ups in the middle of the gym while she tells the rest of the team to run laps along the walls. The coach ridicules the athlete for making a "stupid mistake." At the end of practice the athlete who had done push-ups returns with her father, and they both approach the coach. Coach Rentschler tells the father that if his daughter wants to be a winner, she's going to

have to act less like a child and that if the father doesn't want his daughter to be subjected to this treatment, he can just take his daughter off the team. The coach then storms into the locker room, leaving the athlete in tears and her father standing bewildered.

Later, Coach Rentschler can't believe the low marks Mike has given her on her evaluation in motivation and development of athletes, communication skills, and a number of other areas. She tells Mike that she's coached six of the past nine conference champion volleyball teams, that she's always coached this way, and that she's always had superior evaluations. Later, Mike looks up her records and verifies her claims.

Clearly, Mike's and Coach Rentschler's philosophies about what makes a good volleyball coach differ. Had Mike taken some time early in the year to think about his philosophy, as well as to identify the philosophies of his coaches, he might have realized that there were potential problems. And although identifying conflicting philosophies would have been only the first step in addressing these problems, a clear communication of philosophy was essential to ensure that all athletic department personnel knew in advance the expectations behind the coach evaluations.

Here's how to make philosophy a practical part of your program evaluation system.

Identify your organization's philosophy.   ASEP's philosophy is succinctly expressed by its motto: *Athletes First, Winning Second.* Briefly, this philosophy asserts that, although striving to win is an important part of competition in sport, the physical and emotional development of athletes should never be sacrificed for the sake of winning. What is your organization's philosophy? Complete Exercise 1 now to help you answer this important question (see page 4).

These statements may present similar views of the importance of athletics in your organization, making it easy for you to identify your organization's philosophy. However, you may find that some mission statements identify different priorities, or you may find virtually nothing to help you identify an organizational philosophy. In these cases, determining your organization's philosophy may be more difficult. Whether you have a clear sense of your organization's philosophy or not, you need to take one more step to decide how best to proceed with this information.

Identify your personal philosophy.   Before you can decide how to work with your organization's philosophy, you need to identify your own beliefs about the mission or purpose of athletics. Complete Exercise 2 now to help you with this process (see pages 5–6).

The answers you have just supplied provide a fairly concise look at what you value in your organization's athletic program. As you review these results, you may be wondering how your athletic program can provide these benefits. As a sport director, you may discover that some of the benefits that athletic programs provide for one group directly conflict with those for another group. In addition, this may be the first time you have actually tried to write down how your program offerings should benefit parents, coaches, or athletic trainers. Don't worry! The next section will help you decide what to do with all these priorities.

Identify the fit between organizational and personal philosophies.   Are there conflicts among your own priorities for your organization's athletic program? How closely aligned are your philosophies with those of your organization? It is very important for you to decide how to deal with conflicts between your personal philosophies and those of your organization. As an agent of the organization, you are probably expected to support not only its policies, but also the philosophy behind those policies. Hopefully, you have explored this fit in the interview process and have found a position which allows you to work within your own system of beliefs.

For example, if you believe that participation on interscholastic sports teams should be available to all high school athletes who pursue it, but your organization limits numbers of participants in order to control the ratio of coaches to athletes, and thereby increase the competitiveness of those who actually compete in contests, you have a philosophy conflict with the organization. You will need to decide whether to reconsider your own beliefs, advocate for changes in the organization's philosophy, or work to find other options. In any case, your performance and your expectations for those you supervise will be influenced by your philosophies and those of your organization. In order to approach program evaluation effectively, you will need to reconcile any differences. Use Exercise 3 now to identify potential conflicts of philosophy and to explore ways of dealing with them (see pages 7–8).

Exercise 1: Identifying Your Organization's Philosophy

1. Obtain mission statements, policy manuals, and handbooks for athletics in your school or organization.

2. Examine each item you have collected, looking for statements that identify the mission or primary purpose of athletics in your organization. Many policy manuals and handbooks begin with a section called *Statement of Philosophy* or something similar. These statements express why athletics are part of the organization and/or identify the purpose of the athletic program in the organization. Copy the statements you find onto the following lines.

a. _____

_____

_____

_____

b. _____

_____

_____

_____

c. _____

_____

_____

_____

d. _____

_____

_____

_____

The primary purpose of this exercise is to identify workable strategies when priorities conflict. Too often, these conflicts arise after an evaluation—remember Coach Rentschler? The secondary purpose is to make sure that all athletic program personnel share an understanding of the philosophy behind your expectations before any evaluation takes place. Avoid the temptation to think of these resolution attempts as policies. Instead, think of how you can help those involved with your athletic program understand where conflicts may arise, and provide suggestions of ways to handle those conflicts that promote the integrity of the program, as well as secure the support of all involved. Once you have resolved the potential conflicts between your personal and organizational philosophies, you are ready to communicate that philosophy to others in the form of a resolution statement or motto.

Develop a statement of philosophy or motto. Although it may be difficult to put all these thoughts and values into a brief statement, attempting to do so

Exercise 2: Identifying Your Personal Philosophy

Answer the following questions concerning your personal beliefs about the role of your athletic program.

1. What do you believe to be the most important purposes of your athletic program?

a. _____

b. _____

c. _____

2. Athletic programs are thought to bring a wide range of benefits to their participants. But particular benefits may be more important to some people than they are to others. Rank the following participant benefits for your athletic program offerings, placing the number *1* on the line next to the benefit you feel is most important, the number *2* beside the second most important benefit, and so on to complete the list. If you're like most sport directors, you will have some difficulty because all of these items will seem important. Still, it is very valuable to force yourself to rank them from most to least important. Use the spaces at the bottom of the list for other benefits that you feel are important.

_____ Academic improvement

_____ Competition

_____ Leadership

_____ Physical fitness

_____ Self-esteem

_____ Skill development

_____ Winning

_____ _____

_____ _____

_____ _____

3. What top three benefits should your program provide for coaches?

a. _____

b. _____

c. _____

4. What top three benefits should your program provide for athletic trainers?

a. _____

b. _____

c. _____

5. What top three benefits should your program provide for parents?

a. _____

b. _____

c. _____

6. What top three benefits should your program provide for the community?

a. _____

b. _____

c. _____

can help you refine your beliefs. Here are a few examples to help you get started:

- Athletes First, Winning Second (ASEP's motto)
- Better Athletics Today for a Better Community Tomorrow
- Celebrating the Diversity of the Human Spirit Through Athletics

Notice how each of these statements suggests a different primary purpose. Review your response to the first question of Exercise 2, and see whether you can refine it into a brief philosophy statement or motto for your program. Request input from your colleagues, coaches, athletes—anyone who can help you shape and focus the statement. If you have already developed a statement, reexamine it now in light of this discussion. If you still support the statement, great! The greatest value in producing or revising this statement, though, is that it will provide a foundation upon which to build your program evaluation system. As questions and concerns arise, this statement can provide a starting point for discussion. If your coaches, trainers, and supervisors support your philosophy statement, they can use it as a touchstone to guide their own decisions. Once you have developed this statement, obtain approval from other administrators and appropriate board members. Then include it on your correspondence, memos, and forms to coaches, parents, athletes, and the community as a constant reminder of what is important in your program.

Step 2: Identify Key Roles

Once you have established your philosophy, it's time to identify the scope of your responsibility in program evaluation. Personnel evaluation may be the most important role of your position. Conversely, you may have no formal role in personnel evaluation, only an informal role as a mentor or observer. Regardless of your role, you need to determine how to work with other administrators in the process of evaluating personnel, facilities and equipment, and program offerings. Even if you have primary responsibility, you should seek ways to involve others in the process. Unless you are in a very unusual position, you have more than enough responsibilities to keep you busy. You may seek assistance from coaches, for example, in completing equipment inventories and conducting facility inspections, reporting on the condition of storage areas, and identifying outdated equipment and uniforms taking up valuable storage space. Support staff might duplicate, distribute and collect surveys, collect financial records, and summarize program participation information. Athletic program personnel will be able to assist you in any number of ways, but only if you are in the habit of reviewing which of your tasks can be effectively accomplished by someone else.

While you are thinking about various individuals' roles, consider which personnel to involve in identifying minimum performance standards for your coaches. Either by survey or through representatives, gather input from all supervisors, coaches, trainers, and other appropriate personnel.

Exercise 3:   Reconciling Conflicts Between Personal and Organizational Philosophies

Complete this exercise by looking back at your responses for Exercise 2 and considering conflicts that may arise between your personal and organizational philosophies.

1. Use the first column to write an abbreviated version (two or three words) of the most important purpose and top three benefits you identified for each group in Exercise 2.

2. Next, examine each item you have written in the first column, and look over the purpose as well as the benefits you have listed. Also look back at the organizational philosophy statements you gathered in Exercise 1. Do you see any possible conflicts? For example, if you have identified "leadership" among your top three athletes' benefits and "autonomy in making decisions" among your top three coaches' benefits, conflicts may arise as coaches give up some of their autonomy to provide athletes opportunities to make their own decisions as team leaders. Use the second column to list possible conflicts with each of the items you have listed in the first column.

3. Finally, look at the conflicts you have identified and consider options for resolving them. Using the previous example of a conflict between athletes' leadership and coaches' autonomy, you might identify a resolution option whereby coaches identify in advance specific areas in which they will allow athletes to make decisions. That way, athletes have opportunities to take leadership roles, but coaches maintain their autonomy in leading the team. Use the third column to list options for resolving each of the conflicts you have identified.

Purpose/benefits	Possible conflicts	Resolution options
a. Purpose (from Ex. 2, item 1)		
_____	_____	_____
b. Athletes' benefits (from Ex. 2, item 2)		
_____	_____	_____
_____	_____	_____
_____	_____	_____
c. Coaches' benefits (from Ex. 2, item 3)		
_____	_____	_____
_____	_____	_____
_____	_____	_____
d. Trainers' benefits (from Ex. 2, item 4)		
_____	_____	_____
_____	_____	_____
_____	_____	_____

e. Parents' benefits (from Ex. 2, item 5)

_____   _____   _____

_____   _____   _____

_____   _____   _____

f. Community's benefits (from Ex. 2, item 6)

_____   _____   _____

_____   _____   _____

_____   _____   _____

Discuss the responsibilities of head and assistant coaches' and trainers' positions and come to consensus on what characteristics comprise the minimum acceptable competency for each position. If your evaluation system is to be effective, those who will be held accountable to it need to feel that they had a voice in its creation. We will develop this issue further in the personnel evaluation portion of the guide.

Step 3: Assess Evaluation Needs

Next, you need to determine how many programs and individuals to evaluate and to what extent they need to be evaluated. Use Form 1.1, Identifying Evaluation Needs (see pages 43–44), to assess your program evaluation needs. Make one copy of this form for each of your program offerings. This form provides a good opportunity for you to get into practice obtaining assistance with your evaluation! Consider asking the head coach of each of your sport program offerings to fill out this form and return it to you. When you have completed each of these forms, you will easily be able to determine the number of program offerings and individuals you need to evaluate.

If you are an interscholastic athletic director, you have another important element to consider in assessing evaluation needs: how to evaluate personnel who may also be certified teachers. For example, if you are a middle school athletic director planning to evaluate your personnel and 80% of your coaches are also teachers, they are probably evaluated by your district's teacher evaluation system. You will need to work with your school administration to determine procedures for effectively evaluating these individuals as coaches. If coaching evaluation is an element of a certified teacher's evaluation, the 20% of coaches who are not teachers will not be covered by that process. Careful consideration is important at this point. You have a responsibility to verify that all your coaches—whether they are teachers or not—are safe and perform their duties at a certain level of competency. At the same time, contractual issues and teachers' collective bargaining units may affect your ability to conduct formal evaluations of certified teachers. These agreements frequently specify who has a right to evaluate personnel, as well as the conditions under which evaluations may be performed. You also need to consider how coaches who are not teachers are treated by collective bargaining agreements. Implementing a coaching evaluation program without considering these contractual issues can raise countless barriers to your evaluation efforts. By consulting a teachers' association president along with school administrators early in the process, you not only avoid encountering these barriers, but you also widen your support for meaningful evaluation of coaches and other athletic program personnel.

Step 4: Develop an Evaluation Plan

Now that the early organization is complete, you are ready to develop your program evaluation plan. At this point, you will determine a schedule for conducting your evaluations, as well as how much input will come from you, from supervisors, and from other personnel, athletes, and parents. Use the information you collect from Form 1.1, Identifying Evaluation Needs, to determine the number of personnel, facilities and equipment, and program offerings you will need to evaluate. Refer to the season dates on these forms to determine the best times for evaluating each element of your athletic program. Try to establish a timetable that allows more time than you think you will actually need. That way, if the unexpected should arise—which is likely at some point during the year—you won't be placed in a position of having to disrupt the entire schedule. In addition, keep in mind that it will take some time to record the results of the questionnaires that make up an important part of this evaluation guide (complete discussions of these questionnaires are included in Part Two and Part Three). By planning to receive these forms periodically throughout the year, you can avoid having too much information to manage at any one time. Refer to Table 1.1 (see page 10) for a partial example of a master plan for evaluating an athletic program.

Step 5: Implement the Evaluation Plan

If you have developed your plans carefully, delegated responsibilities appropriately, and communicated expectations clearly, you should be positioned to conduct an efficient and effective program evaluation. During implementation, watch your master plan carefully for signs of difficulty— like unexpected leaves of absence or upcoming heavy workloads that threaten the schedule—and make changes as early as possible. Also monitor the process for unexpected problems and make notes that you can access later to assist you in improving future evaluation efforts. For example, you may find that your hopes for surveying athletic program personnel, athletes, and parents by a certain date are thrown off by a sudden breakdown of a photocopier. Or perhaps a number of your coaches have been misinterpreting your instructions for inspecting facilities. As these problems occur, place brief notes to yourself in a file folder—possibly labeled "Evaluation Challenges"—to provide a reminder to obtain copies further in advance of when you need them and to communicate your expectations for facilities inspection more clearly next year.

Step 6: Review and Revise the Evaluation Plan

As you implement your evaluation plan, and once you have completed your program evaluation, it is important to reflect on your evaluation efforts. What problems did you have? How might you avoid revisiting those problems in the future? What modifications arose that might be worth formalizing into your evaluation system? Organizations tend to change slowly, but they can and do change. Examine your evaluation efforts regularly to ensure that they still accomplish their goals.

 ## SUMMARY

You have worked through a six-step process in preparation for conducting an effective program evaluation. You have moved from considering personal and organizational philosophies to being ready to implement an evaluation plan that uses these philosophies as a guide to make decisions about the quality of your personnel, facilities and equipment, and program offerings. You have also reflected briefly on how to prepare to review and revise your program evaluation plan. It sounds like you're ready, so let's move on to Part Two, which will help you evaluate your athletic program personnel.

Table 1.1   Sample Master Program Evaluation Plan

August	September	October
• Meet with Coaching Committee • Begin football evaluation • Begin volleyball evaluation • Begin cross-country evaluation		• Meet with Coaching Committee • Begin girls' basketball evaluation • Begin boys' basketball evaluation • Begin wrestling evaluation

November	December	January
• Evaluate trainers • Evaluate supervisors • Evaluate support staff	• Meet with Coaching Committee • Evaluate intramural programs	• Evaluate program offerings • Begin girls' track and field evaluation • Begin boys' track and field evaluation • Begin softball evaluation • Begin baseball evaluation

February	March	April
• Meet with Coaching Committee • Begin swimming evaluation		• Meet with Coaching Committee • Evaluate facilities • Evaluate equipment

May	June	July
• Form new Coaching Committee • Review and revise program evaluation plan	• Meet with Coaching Committee	

Part Two

Personnel Evaluation

Let's face it: Evaluating personnel is tricky business. Whether you are the education director of an Olympic national governing body or the athletic director of a small school district, you have a responsibility to ensure that your coaches, trainers, and other personnel meet certain minimum performance expectations. At the same time, you don't want personnel to work only at the level minimally required to keep their jobs. That means you have the added responsibility for educating and motivating your personnel to reach higher and higher levels of skill. Part Two of this guide will provide the tools you need to succeed in these important areas of personnel evaluation.

TROUBLES WITH CHECKLISTS

Let's start by looking at the instruments generally available for evaluating personnel. If you have been directing or coaching for any length of time, you are probably familiar with the checklists most widely used to evaluate coaches. Some coaches are rated as good, excellent, and superior; others occasionally are rated as needs improvement or even poor.

If you collected samples of different checklists from across the country, you would find that the quality varies considerably. Even the best, however, suffer from certain constraints inherent in the check-

list form as an evaluation tool. But let's not be overly negative. These summative instruments—the common term used to refer to forms that rely on observations of individuals performing their duties to arrive at a ranking along a continuum—accomplish certain goals quite well. These forms enable busy sport directors to gain information quickly on the critical components of an individual's work with athletes. This information can then be used to determine whether the person adheres to policies for safety, performs required duties, and interacts appropriately with others. The best summative instruments list specific observable behaviors and include input from the individuals who will be evaluated on them. On these high-quality summative instruments, the difference between a coach who is excellent and one who is superior has been clearly defined, again using descriptions of specific observable behaviors.

Even these high-quality summative evaluation processes often fall short of accomplishing much by way of professional growth. A typical instrument, for example, assigns a number to each category used to describe a coach's performance. From deficient to superior, a coach might score anywhere from 0 to 5 in each of 20 behaviors. At the end of the form is a place for totaling the coach's score. This total is used to assign the coach's overall performance to one of these same five categories. Coaches rated in the lowest categories might be dismissed or remediated, whereas those in the other categories are encouraged to work to improve upon those items for which they have been ranked below superior, with the aim eventually of scoring a 5 on every item, a perfect 100 overall. Professional growth on these instruments is measured by a coach's ability to obtain a higher score by striving to improve upon behaviors rated below superior. Unfortunately, evaluations conducted at different times and by different administrators frequently produce different ratings. Furthermore, evaluators seldom work with coaches to identify strategies for growing professionally. Rather, the results on summative evaluation forms are generally provided to coaches, who are then left to decide for themselves what, if anything, they should do differently.

Of course, few are surprised to discover that the good intentions behind these summative instruments seldom produce, in and of themselves, highly motivated, professional coaching staffs. More often, quarrels erupt over which coaches were identified as excellent versus superior or whether poorly timed observations led to lower scores than coaches felt accurately depicted their performances. Even in the absence of open disagreement, a general feeling of distrust surrounds the process. The idea that a score obtained as the result of a director's brief visit to one practice session can accurately classify the quality of coaching is more than most coaches, and sport directors, are willing to accept. Few coaches and directors feel comfortable moving from the descriptors on a summative evaluation form to intrinsically motivated professional growth. Instead, summative approaches to personnel evaluation tend to be viewed by sport directors and their personnel as a necessary, but not particularly valuable, exercise.

Fortunately, once the primary problem behind the summative evaluation process is recognized, the solution becomes apparent. The sport director's checklist is an important part of the evaluation process, but to be effective, it must be recognized as only one part. A quick example will illustrate.

Picture an individual trying to hang a picture on the wall. Her toolbox contains a couple of screwdrivers, a pair of pliers, and an adjustable wrench, but not a hammer. She pounds the nail with the handle of a screwdriver, but has trouble hitting it squarely and with sufficient force to drive it very far into the wall stud. After bending the nail several times and smashing a few fingers, the handle of the screwdriver cracks and falls apart. If only she had a hammer! Sport directors who approach personnel evaluation without the proper tools face a similar problem. Their summative instruments are very good at identifying unsafe coaches and those who don't fulfill their duties, but they are very poor at motivating coaches. Instead of bent nails and smashed fingers, these sport directors end up with disgruntled coaches and high turnover rates. The continued use of the wrong tool for the job may result in the kind of distrust that makes evaluation a dreaded and ineffectual chore, not an exercise in program enhancement.

SOLUTIONS FROM EDUCATORS

Since the early 1980s, personnel evaluation has received significant attention from experts in educational administration, and the need for separating performance assessment (verifying duty proficiency and safety) from performance enhancement (pro-

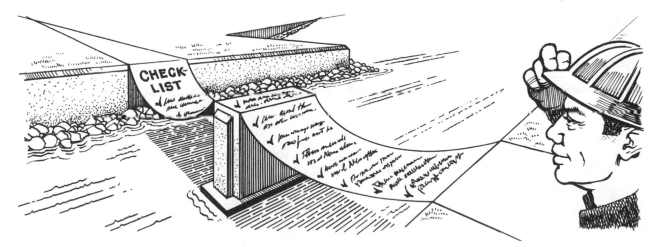

moting professional growth and development) has been recognized. Part Two of this guide has been inspired by a number of educational researchers who have developed, implemented, and studied approaches to personnel evaluation that enable administrators not only to verify the safety and minimum competence of their staffs, but also to increase individuals' sense of intrinsic motivation and promote professional growth and development. When implemented properly, these approaches assist administrators in developing better qualified staff members who are more strongly committed to their organizations.

Many of these approaches to performance assessment and enhancement fall under a category commonly known as formative evaluation, which refers to a process of interaction between an individual and his or her supervisor that focuses on identifying goals and working together not only to determine whether those goals are ultimately achieved, but also to identify the path most likely to lead to success. Rather than building from a checklist, as summative evaluations do, formative evaluations build from a set of goals. An individual setting his or her own goals is much more likely to make an effort to achieve those goals. In the best formative evaluation systems, the supervisor helps the individual refine and prioritize his or her goals, then the supervisor and individual being evaluated work together to achieve the goals. Although formative evaluation instruments aren't solutions for every situation, they are much better tools for promoting professional growth than their summative counterparts.

TOOLS FOR EVALUATING ATHLETIC PROGRAM PERSONNEL

Because different personnel evaluation objectives can best be met by using specialized tools, this section borrows both from summative and formative evaluation systems. You will find the personnel evaluation tools on pages 45–85. Select your choice of tools based on the objectives you have in evaluating personnel, as well as the kind of information

you would like to obtain. For example, when you wish to verify the safety and duty competence of your coaches, select Forms 2.1, 2.2, 2.3, 2.4, and 2.5, which are summative evaluation forms that will help you collect information through your own direct observation of coaches, from the observations of colleagues, athletes, and parents, and even from coaches' own assessments. Specific instructions for conducting your personnel evaluation appear later in Part Two, but a glance at Table 2.1 (see page 14) provides an overview of the tools discussed in this section of the book. As you can see, these tools are designed to assist you in evaluating coaches and in achieving five goals:

- To assure safety in working with athletes
- To assure proficiency in carrying out coaching duties
- To assure administrative competence
- To promote professional growth
- To promote intrinsic motivation

The first three goals have been conceived to cover the minimum competencies of a member of your organization's coaching staff. The first form, the Summative Coach Evaluation Instrument, is built upon the summative approach described previously. However, to overcome the difficulties inherent in instruments which attempt to rank coaches across several categories of performance (poor, average, excellent, superior, etc.), this form requires a simple yes or no response (and a ? option in case the answer is not easily obtained during the observation). Once you have achieved consensus on the specific descriptors of a coach who meets the minimum performance expectations, you no longer need to use this form to determine to what extent a coach exceeds those standards.

Because your coaches interact with a number of individuals, this guide also provides tools specifically designed to gather information about coaches' performance from you, the sport director (Form 2.1, Summative Coach Evaluation Instrument), as well as colleagues (Form 2.2, Colleague Questionnaire), athletes (Form 2.3, Athlete Questionnaire), parents (Form 2.4, Parent Questionnaire), and the coaches themselves (Form 2.5, Coach Self-Appraisal Form). As Table 2.1 shows, different tools have been developed for collecting each type of information. Even so, the surveys and coach questionnaire are

Table 2.1   Personnel Evaluation Tools

Goals	Data source	Collection tools
• Safety assurance • Duty proficiency • Administrative competence	Sport directors	Form 2.1—Summative Coach Evaluation Instrument
	Colleagues	Form 2.2—Colleague Questionnaire
	Athletes	Form 2.3—Athlete Questionnaire
	Parents	Form 2.4—Parent Questionnaire
	Individual under evaluation	Form 2.5—Coach Self-Appraisal Form
• Professional growth • Intrinsic motivation	Individual under evaluation	Form 2.6—Goal Identification Form
	Individual under evaluation Sport directors	Form 2.7—Goal-Setting Conference Form Form 2.8—Progress Appraisal Conference Form
• All goals	Sport directors	Form 2.9—Personnel Evaluation Summary Form

designed around the same basic questions. Questions which appear on multiple instruments have been presented in a consistent order to make it easy for you to compare responses about a coach's performance from one source of information to another.

Finally, to achieve goals of promoting professional growth and intrinsic motivation, a series of forms comprise the formative evaluation component of the guide (Forms 2.6, Goal Identification Form; 2.7, Goal-Setting Conference Form; and 2.8, Progress Appraisal Conference Form). These forms lead sport directors and coaches step by step through the formative evaluation process, starting with setting goals and ending with a formal review of progress toward achieving those goals.

PROCEDURES FOR CONDUCTING YOUR PERSONNEL EVALUATION

Now it's time to take the next big step and begin the process of evaluating your athletic program personnel. Let's begin with your primary area of responsibility in personnel evaluation: coaches.

Evaluating Coaches

Because coaches represent the greatest personnel evaluation need for most sport directors, this guide has been designed with a heavy emphasis on conducting those evaluations. However, you will also find a section to assist you in evaluating trainers, supervisors, and other support staff (see Evaluating Trainers, Supervisors, and Support Staff, pp. 21–23).

Develop Statement of Philosophy or Motto

As you may recall, the first of six steps for effective program evaluation, presented previously in this guide on page 2, involves reflecting on personal and organizational philosophies. If you have not yet developed a statement of philosophy or motto, refer to the discussion on pages 2–6 and take this important first step. Once you have developed this statement, you can focus on the specific goals for your personnel evaluation process.

As you saw in Table 2.1, this book has been designed to help you accomplish five specific goals (see page 14). Take a few minutes to reflect on how each of these goals supports your philosophy statement. For example, ASEP's Athletes First, Winning Second philosophy statement guides our interpretation of these five goals. Minimum competency in safety assurance means that coaches make the safety of athletes their highest priority, that they do not engage in behaviors that risk the safety of athletes for the sake of winning or other personal objectives. Minimum competency in duty proficiency means that coaches possess the skills to promote the physical and emotional development of athletes and that these efforts provide the foundation on which season plans are built. Take a few moments to write down how your philosophy statement is interpreted by the five goals in the personnel evaluation section of this guide.

Philosophy statement: _____

_____

Safety assurance interpretation: _____

_____

Duty proficiency interpretation: _____

_____

Administrative competence interpretation: _____

_____

Professional growth interpretation: _____

_____

Intrinsic motivation interpretation: _____

_____

Identify Roles of Sport Director, Supervisors, and Coaches

Once you have developed your statement of philosophy or motto and expressed how it is interpreted through your personnel evaluation goals, you will be ready to determine your own role in evaluating coaches, as well as how much assistance you can expect from assistants or coach supervisors. The most important action you can take in this step of the process is involving coaches in determining the behaviors that are essential for assuring safety in working with athletes, performing duties with proficiency, and handling administrative duties competently. Personnel will be involved in identifying their own behaviors and goals for professional growth and intrinsic motivation, so at this point focus solely on identifying behaviors that represent the minimum competencies for your coaches.

Assemble a Coaching Committee, comprised of a group of individuals who represent all appropriate personnel. The primary purpose of this committee is to identify the minimum competencies to which all your coaches will be held accountable. Be sure to include individuals from diverse backgrounds. If you work in a school district, for example, you would be wise to involve an active member of the teachers' association. By involving all these stakeholders in the process of identifying coaches' minimum competencies, you will face fewer difficulties when you move to the point of holding coaches accountable. Although the composition of this committee will vary from one setting to another, consider whether yours should include each of the following representatives (male and female, individuals from diverse racial and ethnic backgrounds, and individuals with disabilities):

- Coaches
- Trainers
- Supervisors
- Board members
- Other administrators
- Personnel outside the athletic department
- Representatives of collective bargaining units
- Athletes
- Parents
- Other members of the community

As the previous example with Mike and Coach Rentschler demonstrates, it's essential that all staff members share an understanding of what behaviors represent appropriate minimum competence. Form 2.1, Summative Coach Evaluation Instrument (see pp. 45–55), is the most important instrument to develop in conjunction with your Coaching Committee. This tool, the specific use of which will be covered later in this section, is your primary source for evaluating whether coaches are meeting your minimum performance standards. The version which appears in this guide is probably longer than can be practically managed during a formal coach evaluation. Form 2.1 has been developed to be as comprehensive as possible, with the understanding that you will delete those items which your Coaching Committee feels are not necessary, add items that are appropriate for your needs, and revise items as needed. Because every sport director's needs are different, it is important to customize tools for your unique situation.

Once you have made appropriate modifications to Form 2.1, Summative Coach Evaluation Instrument, take a similar approach with the surveys and questionnaires. Again, because these tools are designed to help you gather information about your coaches, you need to provide your Coaching Committee with a voice in determining which items are most appropriate. To complete this portion of the personnel evaluation process, have your Coaching Committee evaluate Forms 2.2, Colleague Questionnaire; 2.3, Athlete Questionnaire; 2.4, Parent Questionnaire; and 2.5 Coach Self-Appraisal Form (see pages 56–75).

Assess Personnel Evaluation Needs

Before you can begin to implement your personnel evaluation process, you need to gather information on the number of coaches you have to evaluate, as well as identify the groups of individuals to receive questionnaires. At this point, identify the total number of coaches to evaluate; the staff members to receive Form 2.2, the Colleague Questionnaire; and the approximate number of athletes and parents to receive Forms 2.3, Athlete Questionnaire and 2.4, Parent Questionnaire (see pages 56–72).

An important reason for taking this step now is to identify the appropriate method for distributing and collecting the questionnaires. To encourage honest responses on questionnaires, it is important to assure anonymity to the individuals who complete them. Not only does this assurance require you to avoid asking for names on the forms, but it also includes providing a method for returning questionnaires without the possibility of being identified. Although using return envelopes provides a high degree of security, it may also require high postage costs and staff time for adequate preparation. A collection box may provide an acceptable alternative, but it may reduce the number of questionnaires returned by parents. An approach which might overcome these limitations is to distribute forms to athletes and parents a week or two before an awards ceremony, then ask them to bring the forms for deposit in a collection box there. If you also make additional forms available at the ceremony for those who have lost or forgotten their originals, you may increase the total number of forms returned. No matter which way you proceed, emphasize the anonymity of responses by including instructions for their return on the forms. Any approach you select will provide advantages and disadvantages, but the best approach can only be determined if you understand your needs for the entire year. Don't feel like all responsibility for assessing needs falls on your shoulders. Involve your Coaching Committee to make this aspect of personnel evaluation more manageable and to provide the greatest opportunity for developing creative solutions.

Develop a Personnel Evaluation Plan

You have communicated your philosophy, determined your role and involved appropriate stakeholders, customized your evaluation tools, and assessed your needs. Now you need to develop a master plan for evaluating personnel. In addition to the planning you have already finished, sit down with a calendar and the copies of Form 1.1, Identifying Evaluation Needs, which you developed in Part One of the guide (see pages 8–9). Then establish a schedule for conducting your personnel evaluation. Table 1.1 (see page 10) provided an example of an evaluation plan for the entire program. Table 2.2 provides an example of an evaluation plan specifically for personnel. Ideally, you should begin this process near the end of one year in preparation for the next year. That way, you will be able to plan every step: organizing the following year's Coaching Committee, initial meetings with personnel, observations of coaches, distribution and collection of questionnaires, dates for the formative evaluation process (see pages 29–31 for a complete discussion of the formative evaluation process), and dates for evaluating the personnel evaluation process. Allow more time than you think you will need. The unexpected can complicate even the most detailed plans. If you plan for delays, you will be able to maintain your schedule, and more importantly, your sanity!

Implement the Personnel Evaluation Plan

Now just follow the plan you have established. As you implement your plan, watch for unexpected complications and modify the plan accordingly. Unforeseen travel, for example, might take you or a coach away at a time scheduled for a meeting. When schedules are especially tight—at the very beginning or end of seasons, for example—rescheduling one step might delay other steps in your evaluation process. If you recognize these conflicts in advance you will be much less likely to find yourself pressed for time to meet deadlines in your evaluation process. Take a few minutes at the beginning of each week to determine whether planned activities are on schedule and to incorporate newly scheduled events and obligations into the existing plan.

Review and Revise the Personnel Evaluation Plan

As challenges to your plans arise, keep a file of notes that you can assemble toward the end of the year to modify future personnel evaluation plans. When helpful, bring these notes to the attention of the Coaching Committee to obtain input on how best

Table 2.2   Sample Personnel Evaluation Plan

	August	September
Week 1	• Meet with Coaching Committee • Meet with supervisors and support staff (distribute Form 2.6)	• Observe football coaches (complete Form 2.1)
Week 2	• Preseason meeting with all coaches (distribute Form 2.6)	• Observe volleyball coaches (complete Form 2.1)
Week 3		• Observe cross-country coaches (complete Form 2.1)
Week 4	• Goal-Setting Conference with football, volleyball, and cross-country coaches (complete Form 2.7)	

	October	November
Week 1	• Meet with Coaching Committee • Goal-Setting Conference with girls' and boys' basketball, wrestling coaches (complete Form 2.7)	• Collect and review Forms 2.2–2.5 for football
Week 2	• Distribute Colleague, Athlete, Parent, and Self-Appraisal Forms (2.2–2.5) for head football coach	• Collect and review Forms 2.2–2.5 for volleyball
Week 3	• Distribute Colleague, Athlete, Parent, and Self-Appraisal Forms (2.2–2.5) for head volleyball coach	• Collect and review Forms 2.2–2.5 for cross-country
Week 4	• Distribute Colleague, Athlete, Parent, and Self-Appraisal Forms (2.2–2.5) for head cross-country coach	• Goal-Setting Conference with trainers, supervisors, and support staff (complete Form 2.7)

	December	January
Week 1	• Meet with Coaching Committee • Goal-Setting Conference with intramural program coaches (complete Form 2.7)	
Week 2	• Observe girls' basketball coaches (complete Form 2.1)	• Goal-Setting Conference with girls' track and field coaches (complete Form 2.7)
Week 3	• Observe boys' basketball coaches (complete Form 2.1)	• Goal-Setting Conference with boys' track and field coaches (complete Form 2.7)
Week 4	• Observe wrestling coaches (complete Form 2.1)	• Goal-Setting Conference with softball coaches (complete Form 2.7)

	February	March
Week 1	• Meet with Coaching Committee • Goal-Setting Conference with baseball coaches (complete Form 2.7)	• Collect and review Forms 2.2–2.5 for girls' basketball
Week 2	• Goal-Setting Conference with swimming coaches (complete Form 2.7) • Distribute Colleague, Athlete, Parent, and Self-Appraisal Forms (2.2–2.5) for head girls' basketball coach	• Collect and review Forms 2.2–2.5 for boy's basketball
Week 3	• Distribute Colleague, Athlete, Parent, and Self-Appraisal Forms (2.2–2.5) for head boys' basketball coach	• Observe girls' track and field coaches (complete Form 2.1) • Collect and review Forms 2.2–2.5 for wrestling
Week 4	• Distribute Colleague, Athlete, Parent, and Self-Appraisal Forms (2.2–2.5) for head wrestling coach	• Observe boys' track and field coaches (complete Form 2.1) • Progress Appraisal Conference for football coaches (complete Form 2.8)

(continued)

Table 2.2   *(continued)*

	April	May
Week 1	• Meet with Coaching Committee • Observe softball coaches (complete Form 2.1) • Progress Appraisal Conference for volleyball coaches (complete Form 2.8)	• Distribute Colleague, Athlete, Parent, and Self-Appraisal Forms (2.2–2.5) for head baseball coach • Collect and review Forms 2.2–2.5 for girls' and boys' track and field • Progress Appraisal Conference for wrestling coaches (complete Form 2.8)
Week 2	• Observe baseball coaches (complete Form 2.1) • Distribute Colleague, Athlete, Parent, and Self-Appraisal Forms (2.2–2.5) for head girls' track and field coach • Progress Appraisal Conference for cross-country coaches (complete Form 2.8)	• Form new Coaching Committee • Distribute Colleague, Athlete, Parent, and Self-Appraisal Forms (2.2–2.5) for head swimming coach • Collect and review Forms 2.2–2.5 for softball and baseball • Progress Appraisal Conference for boys' and girls' track and field coaches (complete Form 2.8)
Week 3	• Observe swimming coaches (complete Form 2.1) • Distribute Colleague, Athlete, Parent, and Self-Appraisal Forms (2.2–2.5) for head boys' track and field coach • Progress Appraisal Conference for girls' basketball coaches (complete Form 2.8)	• Collect and review Forms 2.2–2.5 for swimming • Progress Appraisal Conference for softball, baseball, and swimming coaches (complete Form 2.8)
Week 4	• Distribute Colleague, Athlete, Parent, and Self-Appraisal Forms (2.2–2.5) for head softball coach • Progress Appraisal Conference for boys' basketball coaches (complete Form 2.8)	• Progress Appraisal Conference for trainers, supervisors, and support staff (complete Form 2.8) • Summarize personnel evaluation (complete Form 2.9)

	June	July
Week 1	• Meet with Coaching Committee • Prepare personnel evaluation plan for next year	
Week 2		
Week 3		
Week 4		

to meet these challenges and to reduce the likelihood of problems arising in the future. Once your evaluation process is complete, you are ready to begin planning for an even better next year!

Evaluating Trainers, Supervisors, and Support Staff

Evaluation of noncoaching personnel is likely to differ in some significant ways from evaluation of coaches. These individuals fulfill fundamentally different roles than coaches. Whereas a coach is responsible for developing season objectives, practice plans, and working closely with athletes during every practice and contest, other staff members tend to serve roles which enhance the ability of the sport director and coaching staff to perform their duties. While trainers may share responsibility for promoting athletes' safety, few sport directors are clinically qualified to observe trainers' techniques to determine their levels of competency.

Although the nature of evaluation for these individuals differs, the need to evaluate them still exists. Consult your Coaching Committee to determine the appropriate method of evaluating these individuals. Although a summative observation instrument like Form 2.1, Summative Coach Evaluation Instrument (see pages 45–55), is seldom appropriate, you may be able to identify certain aspects of the form that could be adapted for use in evaluating these individuals. Questionnaires may be appropriate, too. Just follow the same process

with these staff members as you do in developing your coach evaluation plan. The Coaching Committee can help you determine the best summative approach for your setting, but you can make the process more effective by first thinking through a few issues. Let's look at some specific considerations for conducting summative evaluations of trainers, supervisors, and support staff.

Evaluating Athletic Trainers

Since you may not have the clinical expertise to determine through directly observing their techniques whether your athletic trainers are performing their duties properly, think about other ways to determine whether these individuals are proficient. Ask questions like these:

• Do trainers follow the recommendations of physicians?

• Do athletes' minor injuries heal, or does continued participation increase the severity of the injury?

• Are accident report forms completed properly and on time?

• Do trainers provide attention to all athletes or only to the most gifted athletes?

• Do athletes understand their roles in facilitating the healing of injuries?

• Do trainers recognize and address patterns of injury that arise during the season?

By asking these kinds of questions—and others that your Coaching Committee decides are appropriate—you can gain some insight into the performance of your athletic trainers. Just as seeking input from multiple sources is important in evaluating coaches, you should collect information about your trainers from coaches, parents, and athletes.

Evaluating Supervisors

If you are among those sport directors who are fortunate enough to have the assistance of supervisors for managing your athletic program personnel, you need to determine whether these individuals are proficient in carrying out their duties. As a sport director, you are likely to be able to determine what actions constitute proficiency in a supervisor; these duties largely parallel your own. Still, collecting this information through direct observation can be difficult and in some cases even intrusive. An effective way to gather information for evaluating your supervisors is to design questionnaires to be completed by the individuals for whom these supervisors have responsibility. Follow the format of Form 2.3, Athlete Questionnaire (see pages 67–69), and obtain answers to questions like these:

- Do supervisors provide personnel with clear, constructive feedback?

- Do supervisors encourage personnel to ask questions and share ideas?

- Do supervisors follow through with agreements or promises?

- Do supervisors show a genuine interest in helping all personnel succeed?

- Do supervisors meet deadlines for submitting reports?

- Do supervisors complete reports that are clear and sufficiently detailed?

As you did with coaches, begin by determining the minimum competencies for your supervisors; then design questionnaires that specifically address those competencies. The questions presented previously are designed to address general responsibilities of most supervisors, but they may not be appropriate for everyone. For example, if your program is very large, you may have a supervisor in charge of public relations, another in charge of facilities and equipment, and a third in charge of personnel. To design one questionnaire to address the minimum competencies for all three of these individuals may not be the most effective way to assess whether they are performing their duties proficiently. You might even decide that a questionnaire is not appropriate for meeting your needs. No matter what situation you face, involving your Coaching Committee in determining the best evaluation approach to take with supervisors will help ensure that evaluations of all individuals are designed to promote the philosophy of your program.

Evaluating Support Staff

Similar to athletic trainers and supervisors, support staff's performance is often difficult to assess through direct observation. Once again, you may decide to design a questionnaire to collect information from individuals who interact with these personnel on a regular basis. You may even be the person who has the most frequent contact with support staff. Regardless of whether you decide to develop a questionnaire or monitor support staff's performance through your regular interaction with them, you should determine minimum competencies for these individuals. Here are some questions to help you begin thinking about the duty proficiency of support staff:

- Are duties performed in a timely fashion?

- Is communication with athletic department staff and others conducted professionally?

- Are priorities followed appropriately?

- Are records maintained neatly and in an organized fashion?

- Are tasks accomplished neatly and completely?

• Are messages communicated clearly and in a timely fashion?

Regardless of how you decide to conduct summative evaluation for supervisors, trainers, and support staff, the formative evaluation component of this guide (see pages 29–31) is as appropriate for these individuals as it is for coaches. Because the formative evaluation component is designed to provide your personnel with opportunities for growth and to increase intrinsic motivation, follow this process with all personnel.

GUIDELINES FOR EFFECTIVE USE OF PERSONNEL EVALUATION TOOLS

Next, we turn our attention to the proper use of the specific tools in this section of the guide. Because your personnel evaluation plan has been developed with consensus from the Coaching Committee to achieve specific goals, your decision on which instruments to include in that plan should be based upon how these tools can help you achieve your goals. For example, your committee may determine that you should begin by using some of the tools in this guide, then expand to include others in the years that follow. As you may recall from Table 2.1 (see page 14), the tools are developed first to achieve specific goals, then to enhance your ability to collect information from enough sources to arrive at sound conclusions and make recommendations with confidence. While each of these forms provides access to unique information about coaches, you and your Coaching Committee are best situated to decide how best to collect information in your organization and how rapidly you will be able to implement this entire program evaluation approach.

This section of the book has been divided into two distinct components: summative evaluation and formative evaluation. Keep in mind that the most common barriers to effective personnel evaluation have arisen from attempts to make summative evaluation instruments into universal tools. Because each approach to evaluation is effective at accomplishing distinct goals, a comprehensive personnel evaluation system needs to use summative tools for determining minimum competencies and formative tools to promote professional growth and intrinsic motivation. Let's take a closer look at each approach.

Summative Evaluation

By now the term summative evaluation should sound a bit less confusing. Keep in mind that this approach to evaluation is characterized by the checklist that has become such a common feature of most personnel evaluation systems. Summative evaluations are very effective at assisting sport directors in collecting information relating to the minimum competencies of their personnel. By visiting a coach's practice or attending a contest, you can quickly scan a list of behaviors and determine which ones a coach performed and which a coach did not perform. If a coach failed to perform certain essential responsibilities or acted in a manner inconsistent with your organization's policies, you can make note of that on the form. In this way, you can collect more information about a coach's performance without having to attend a large number of practices.

You will notice that Form 2.1, Summative Coach Evaluation Instrument (see pages 45–55), has been divided into three parts. Part I focuses on coaching behaviors relating to safety, Part II on duty proficiency, and Part III on administrative competence. Although all three areas are important for determining the minimum level of competence of your coaches, only the first two parts can be determined through observation. For example, the first item in Part I, "Removes hazards from practice/contest area," is easily observed. However, the first item in Part III, "Attends required district meetings," while an important element for determining whether a coach performs minimum acceptable performance standards, would be difficult to determine through observation. Therefore, to respond to Part III of the form, you need to collect documents to verify your responses. The documents will vary with each organization. To determine the appropriate documentation in your organization, discuss each of these items with your Coaching Committee. For example, returning to the first item in Part III, how do you know whether a coach attends required district meetings? You may decide to check minutes of meetings, to provide in advance a list of coaches who should attend each meeting during the year, or simply to ask coaches which meetings they have attended. Whatever you decide, you need to consult your Coaching Committee at the outset to determine what will be appropriate documentation for each of these items in Part III.

If you have assistance as a sport director, you might be able to delegate one or more portions of the summative evaluation to supervisors or other assistants. Bring this issue to the attention of the Coaching Committee to ensure that everyone understands the responsibilities that will be delegated.

When you first arrive at a practice or contest, try to find a location that will not draw attention away from the coach. Your presence may distract athletes, so try to minimize this distraction. Be sure to take a few moments to fill in the information at the top of Form 2.1. This form will be an official record of your observation, and should it lead to the sanctioning of a coach, you need to be confident that the information is correct.

Form 2.1 has been organized to the extent possible to present descriptions of behaviors in the order that they typically occur during a practice or contest. By familiarizing yourself in advance with the items included on the form, you should be able to spend most of your time observing the practice or contest, not trying to find descriptors on the form.

As mentioned earlier, problems with summative evaluation forms have arisen largely from attempts at using them to promote professional growth. Even when these forms have been developed with the best intentions, ranking coaches on scales and categorizing their performance as poor, good, excellent, and superior can create conflicts and distrust. Form 2.1 overcomes this weakness of traditional tools by simplifying the responses, making them more objective. Instead of stating that a coach's actions for "Removes hazards from practice/contest area"—the first item on the form—are poor, good, excellent, or superior, the form simply reports whether the coach does or does not remove them, then provides an area for a statement describing the specific observation of the coach that prompted the response. Although the kinds of performances listed on the form are typical of these instruments, the rating scale has been replaced with three simple responses. If you observe a coach exhibiting a performance, circle "yes." If the coach fails to exhibit the performance, circle "no." Of course, sometimes you aren't able to determine whether a certain performance has been exhibited. For example, if you arrived for an observation after practice had already begun, you might not know whether the coach inspected the facility for hazards. In this case, you would circle "?" to indicate that you were unable to determine whether this performance was exhibited.

Form 2.1 has also been designed to encourage you to make notes that will assist you in verifying the accuracy of your appraisal of the coach's performance. As you can see, for each item we have provided a box labeled "Observations" ("Documentation" in Part III). If you observe a coach checking for frayed cables on weight machines, you might circle "yes" for the second item, "Inspects equipment for hazards." Then, in the box labeled "Observations," you could write that you observed the coach inspecting those cables. These descriptions of the coach's behavior are especially important for any "no" or "?" responses you might make. For example, if your baseball coach introduces the proper technique for sliding into a base, but fails to warn athletes of potential dangers in doing so, you might circle "no" to item 5, "Warns athletes of inherent risks of activities." To provide evidence that your response is more than just an opinion, you should be sure to describe what the coach did in introducing the skill, noting that she or he did not warn athletes. Should this issue become a source of controversy, your written record of the actual events as they occurred will serve you much better than relying on your memory.

Once you have completed your observation, look closely at the items for which you were unable to respond "yes" or "no." If there are a number of these items, or if you have been unable to respond to an item that you feel uncomfortable leaving undetermined, you may need to arrange for follow-up observations. As you circle the "?" response, be sure to make note of why you were unable to observe the indicated behavior. A large number of "?" responses may indicate the need for follow-up observations, but only by documenting your reasons for these responses can you show why you did or did not decide to follow up. Discuss this issue with your Coaching Committee to identify general guidelines to follow in these instances.

At the end of your observation, you might wish to leave the coach a note that expresses your gratitude for his or her acceptance of your intrusion. Personally hand the note to the coach only if you may do so without disrupting the practice. Otherwise, consider the best location to ensure that only the coach will have access to the note. In some cases, for example, only a mailbox will do. These notes help reduce the anxiety that coaches sometimes feel after observations without forcing you to provide immediate feedback on the quality of the coach's performance. You might also include a statement that you'll be getting in touch to schedule a conference to discuss the results of the evaluation.

It is important to hold a conference following the summative evaluation observation so that your coaches know how they have performed. Begin by highlighting those behaviors that you found particularly effective at achieving the organization's goals. Then, point out areas for which you circled "no." As you do so, avoid using statements that blame the coach; instead, try to phrase your observations as objectively as possible. For example, instead of saying, "You didn't give the athletes enough water," try a statement like, "Some of the athletes showed signs of possible heat stress. It was pretty hot and humid, and under those conditions athletes could lose as much as a couple of quarts of sweat in an hour. They could have used frequent water breaks under those extreme conditions." Be prepared to discuss the implications of these comments, as well as the coach's perceptions of his or her own performance. Attempt to keep an open mind. Allow the coach a chance to respond to your appraisal. Focus the conference on your mutual interest in the physical and emotional development of athletes, and emphasize your interest in working with the coach to help him or her succeed.

Of course, Form 2.1 isn't perfect. Sometimes you visit a coach on a bad day. Sometimes a coach who knows an evaluation is coming will alter behaviors

to look better. To reduce the impact of these limitations, schedule more than one observation during the season. Try to observe the coach at different points during the season, and consider observing contests as well as practices. Unannounced observations are often viewed as more authentic ways of gaining accurate views of a coach's performance. However, if you decide these unannounced visits are an important element in your coach evaluation process, be sure that doing so will not create a contractual problem. Also, be sure to visit all coaches unexpectedly so that you cannot be accused of picking on one coach. Most importantly, bring this issue before your Coaching Committee at the beginning of the process so that everyone understands the motivation behind these surprise visits. If your Coaching Committee agrees that they represent a valuable element in your evaluation plan, you can reduce the likelihood that these visits will generate feelings of distrust among your coaches.

The summative evaluation instruments in this guide have been designed to further reduce the likelihood that limitations of the observation process—like the limited amount of time you have to spend directly observing coaches' practices—interfere with your ability to conduct an effective personnel evaluation. By using the questionnaires—Forms 2.2, Colleague Questionnaire; 2.3, Athlete Questionnaire; 2.4, Parent Questionnaire; and 2.5, Coach Self-Appraisal Form (see pages 56–75)—you can collect information regarding coaches' performances from a variety of sources, including colleagues, athletes, parents, and the coaches themselves. These questionnaires follow the same approach as Form 2.1, Summative Coach Evaluation Instrument, but contain items more appropriate for their intended audiences. By comparing the results of these various sources of information, you can reach decisions about coaches' competencies with greater confidence. We recommend that you distribute these questionnaires to the widest number of individuals appropriate for each coach. Doing so helps you collect enough information to identify trends in the feedback you receive about your coaches. After distributing questionnaires, you may find that fewer than half are actually returned. By keeping these considerations in mind, you can more easily avoid ending up with too few questionnaires to get good impressions of your coaches. However, because programs vary significantly both in size and available funding, your Coaching Committee should be involved in determining how many forms to distribute.

Although most of these forms are self-explanatory, a few words on Form 2.2, Colleague Questionnaire, might be helpful. This form has been designed to be distributed to a coach's colleagues, including other coaches and, in the case of an interscholastic setting, to teachers. These colleagues will have varying levels of knowledge and interaction with your coaches, but to overlook these individuals as a source of information would be a mistake. Particularly in a school setting, for example, teacher colleagues can provide feedback relating to whether coaches communicate with them about athletes' academic progress. Regardless of how much interaction coaches have with other personnel in the organization, it is important to consider how you might benefit from distributing copies of Form 2.2 to adults in your organization.

Before you copy these questionnaires, be sure to fill in the information at the top of the form, including the coaches' names. This way, you don't have to write on every single form, and you don't have to rely on others to fill in the blanks. To reduce the number of forms that colleagues need to complete, as well as the number you need to copy, Form 2.2 provides space to list four coaches. Be sure that the dates you have included allow sufficient time for reflection and return, but don't allow so much time that the forms can be forgotten. In fact, sometimes a more urgent deadline will motivate people to return your questionnaires. Distribute these questionnaires at the end of the season. Previously in this section, you planned how to distribute and collect these questionnaires (see page 17). Now determine how best to use them.

If you are comfortable using database or spreadsheet software on a computer, you might set up such a form to assist you in tabulating the results of your questionnaires. However, you can do an excellent job with a piece of paper and some planning. Either way, if you are dealing with a large number of questionnaires, you should consider involving support staff in this part of the process. Recording this information is going to take some time, and it may not be appropriate for athletes to have access to these questionnaires, so select a member of your support staff and make sure that individual has time to do a good job. You may find that, while athletes shouldn't

work with these questionnaires, they can still assist by taking over some of the duties that your support staff would typically perform, thereby freeing up time for your support staff to record questionnaire results.

Although a number of approaches for tabulating results would be effective, here's an example to get you started. One of the easiest ways to determine the results of these questionnaires is to start with a blank copy of the questionnaire (an extra copy which already contains the information at the top of the form works well). Write "Summary of Responses" at the top of the sheet. Next, divide each "observations" box into three equal sections. The first section is for "yes" responses, the second section is for "no" responses, and the final section is for "?" responses. Then, simply place the stack of returned questionnaires for a given coach in a pile. Start with the first page of the first questionnaire in the pile, and place a hash or tally mark in the appropriate place on the first page of your summary form. After you have recorded the results of the first page of the first questionnaire, proceed to record the results of the first page of the rest of the stack. Then continue the process for each page until you have tallied all the results (see Figure 2.1 for a sample of a completed portion of Form 2.2, Colleague Questionnaire).

By looking at the total number of "yes," "no," and "?" responses on the "Summary of Responses" sheet, you will be able to determine whether certain categories represent strengths or potential difficulties for a coach. By repeating this process for each of the forms—2.2, Colleague Questionnaire; 2.3, Athlete Questionnaire; and 2.4, Parent Questionnaire—you can also identify whether perceptions of a coach's strengths and weaknesses are shared by colleagues, athletes, and parents. And by comparing these results to those of Form 2.5, Coach Self-Appraisal Form, you can determine whether the coach's perceptions match those of others.

On a separate sheet of paper, list the observations and comments that have been offered for each individual. By recording all of these in one place, you will be able to determine the strengths of each individual, as well as whether certain concerns have been raised by a sufficient number of individuals to warrant further investigation. Compare these comments to the "yes," "no," and "?" responses you have recorded previously, as well as to the results of

Figure 2.1 Sample of a completed portion of Form 2.2, Colleague Questionnaire.

Summary of Responses

COLLEAGUE QUESTIONNAIRE

Please return to: _____   Date distributed: _____

Please return by: _____

Because we believe it essential to work together for the positive development of our athletes, we are requesting that you take a few moments to provide feedback about the coaches whose names appear below. Please submit your comments anonymously. Although the form will not be shared with the coaches, the collective comments of all staff members will be used to assist them in identifying areas for professional growth. Thank you in advance for your time.

To complete the form, circle the response that best describes each coach's performance for each descriptor. If the answer is difficult to determine, or cannot be determined at this time, circle the question mark. In the space below each descriptor, labeled "Observations," write a brief description of the specific performance that led you to circle your response for each coach.

			Coach 1 Johnson	Coach 2 McGrath	Coach 3 Hernandez	Coach 4 Jackson
1. Monitors athletes' academic progress			yes no ?	yes no ?	yes no ?	yes no ?

Y	N	? Observations Y	N		?	
Coach 1 ⅣⅣ ⅣⅣ ⅣⅣ IIII			Coach 2 ⅣⅣ ⅣⅣ ⅣⅣ		ⅣⅣ I	
Coach 3 ⅣⅣ ⅣⅣ III	III	III	Coach 4 ⅣⅣ II	ⅣⅣ ⅣⅣ	II	

	Coach 1 Johnson	Coach 2 McGrath	Coach 3 Hernandez	Coach 4 Jackson
2. Solicits colleagues' input when appropriate	yes no ?	yes no ?	yes no ?	yes no ?

Y	N	? Observations Y	N	?
Coach 1 卌 卌 卌 IIII		**Coach 2** 卌 卌 卌	卌 I	
Coach 3 卌 卌 III	IIII	II　**Coach 4** 卌	卌 卌 II	II

	Coach 1 Johnson	Coach 2 McGrath	Coach 3 Hernandez	Coach 4 Jackson
3. Communicates goals and expectations clearly	yes no ?	yes no ?	yes no ?	yes no ?

Y	N	? Observations Y	N	?
Coach 1 卌 卌 卌 IIII		**Coach 2** 卌 IIII	卌 I	卌 I
Coach 3 卌 IIII	IIII	卌 I　**Coach 4** III	卌 卌 II	IIII

Form 2.1, Summative Coach Evaluation Instrument, for each coach to verify that your appraisal of the coach is accurate.

You should discuss with your Coaching Committee just how much of an impact these questionnaires will have on your formal appraisal of a coach. Some organizations will elect to include all these responses as portions of the formal summative evaluation. Others, however, will only use these questionnaires to identify areas for further growth. As always, make sure that all personnel understand from the beginning the role these questionnaires are to play in the summative evaluation process.

Formative Evaluation

If you hope to promote professional growth and intrinsic motivation in your personnel, you need to move beyond traditional summative evaluation systems. While many sport directors and organizations have worked hard to adapt their summative forms to accomplish these purposes, the instrument is poorly equipped to accomplish the task.

How Does Formative Evaluation Work?

Unlike summative evaluation instruments, which identify specific behaviors and appraise individuals' performances, formative instruments start from a premise that the best way to promote professional growth and intrinsic motivation is to let the individual being evaluated identify the goals to be pursued. A primary criticism of formative instruments is that they fail to identify whether personnel meet minimum levels of competency. Clearly, this charge is made by those searching for a universal tool for evaluation. The formative evaluation is specifically designed to promote professional growth and intrinsic motivation, while the summative evaluation is designed to determine minimum competency. Just as a screwdriver is poorly designed for driving nails, a hammer leaves much to be desired when a screw needs tightening. These evaluative tools together enable their users to accomplish much more than was possible with either alone.

The formative evaluation process consists of the following steps:

- Set goals
- Refine goals and identify strategies to achieve them

- Pursue goals
- Evaluate progress toward achieving goals

Because the personnel being evaluated identify the goals to be pursued, your role in formative evaluation is different than in summative evaluation. As the sport director, you need to be prepared to step back from your role as appraiser and shift more toward the role of mentor. For some sport directors, this process can be difficult, largely due to a lack of experience in taking this role. But with some thought and a little practice, most sport directors find this new role a comfortable one.

The formative evaluation tools in this guide— Forms 2.6, Goal Identification Form; 2.7, Goal-Setting Conference Form; and 2.8, Progress Appraisal Conference Form—are designed to assist you and your personnel in pursuing the process, even if you have never tried it before. Recall that the Coaching Committee needs to be included in determining the role formative evaluation is to play in your personnel evaluation system. If personnel perceive the formative evaluation process as something that is not genuinely provided as a means for assisting them in achieving personal professional development goals, they are unlikely to benefit from the process. As sport director, you can help personnel to embrace the process by asserting its intentions in preseason meetings and by focusing conversations during the process on how you and the individual can work together to achieve that individual's goals. Once personnel begin to reach their goals, intrinsic motivation becomes a strong force compelling them to continue their professional growth and development. After you have read the following description and understood the formative evaluation process, work with your Coaching Committee to achieve consensus on the specific approach you will take to formative evaluation. The following steps are essential for making formative evaluation a valuable component of your athletic program. As you read about each step, the text will explain that step's purpose, as well as what roles you and your personnel should fill.

Set Goals. The process of setting goals can begin as soon as your first personnel meeting of the year. As you discuss the personnel evaluation process, emphasize the value of the formative evaluation component. If you are enthusiastic about its benefits, your personnel will be more likely to follow your lead. Distribute Form 2.6, Goal Identification Form (see pages 76–77), and briefly walk personnel through the process the form presents for identifying goals. Although athletic program personnel will fill in the details later, they will benefit from your initial explanation of the process. As was the case with the questionnaires described previously, be sure to complete the information at the top of the form so that personnel know when they should complete these forms. Instructions have been included on the form, but because the examples are aimed at coaches, you might want to adapt the examples for supervisors, trainers, and support staff. Pay particular attention to Steps 3 and 4, which require personnel to suggest actions for achieving goals. Emphasize your commitment to working with personnel to achieve their goals. You aren't there to make sure the goals are achieved, only to provide appropriate assistance that will facilitate individuals' pursuits of their own goals.

At this point also emphasize that personnel should identify goals that they can work toward over the course of the coming year. Although long-term goals (such as ultimate career goals) can also be placed on Form 2.6, Goal Identification Form, explain that you will be meeting with each individual soon to discuss the process for achieving some goals by the end of the year. Finally, inform personnel that this process will culminate in a meeting toward the end of the year that will present an opportunity to reflect on the process and make plans for the future.

Refine Goals and Identify Strategies to Achieve Them.   Once your personnel have submitted their copies of Form 2.6 you need to take some time to review the goals each individual has identified. Look at their responses to Step 2 and attempt to identify three of the goals that you believe are most

likely to be achieved through the course of the coming year. Next, reflect on the actions identified in Steps 3 and 4 and consider whether you might be able to suggest other ideas to assist personnel in achieving their goals. Now look at Form 2.7, Goal-Setting Conference Form (see pages 78–79). As you refer again to an individual's responses to Form 2.6, think about how you would respond to each of the steps on Form 2.7, particularly Step 4 for establishing criteria for determining goal achievement. This step may provide the greatest difficulty for your personnel, so be ready to offer suggestions to spark constructive thinking.

When you are ready, meet with each individual and work through Form 2.7. Although you will be filling out the information on Form 2.7, avoid the temptation to share all your suggestions first. Remember that the individual needs to feel committed to pursuing these goals; you should offer suggestions only to jump start a slow process or to maintain the focus on the issues at hand. When you get to Step 4 of Form 2.7, emphasize that the individual will not be judged negatively for falling short of achieving goals. The year will bring surprises to you and your personnel, and you both need to recognize that unexpected developments may have an impact on pursuit of goals. The important part of this meeting is leaving you and the individual being evaluated with a clear understanding of what each of you will be doing to work toward achieving these goals.

Pursue Goals.   Although the primary responsibility for achieving goals lies with the individuals who set them, you need to modify your personnel evaluation plan for the year to include the actions listed in Step 3 of Form 2.7 for all personnel. One of the most valuable actions you can take to assist your personnel, particularly your coaches, is to take the role of impartial observer. One of the greatest challenges for coaches is the amount of time spent working with athletes without the benefit of other adults' feedback on the coach's own day-to-day performance. Even when assistant coaches and trainers are present, these adults seldom have the opportunity to work together to help each other improve their performance. Help your personnel determine whether they are making progress by offering to observe them in practices and contests. Instead of appraising overall performance, identify specific aspects of behavior to look for. Avoid commenting on the quality of performance and instead attempt to record what you have seen. For example, if a coach has identified a goal of improving her communication with athletes, avoid the temptation to write whether she was effective. Instead, as closely as possible write what she said and how the athletes responded. Think of your observation as an exercise in writing a script. You just want to record events. If the individual feels comfortable, you might also offer to video or audio tape performance.

Regardless of how you decide to record your observations, schedule a follow up meeting. At that meeting, share your observations and ask questions to guide him or her toward a better understanding of what happened. Ask questions like these:

- What was going through your mind when Tami said that?

- What did you want to happen next?

- What else do you think you might have been able to say or do?

These questions will not only help the individual understand the situation but will also help develop trust, which can promote further progress in the future.

Evaluate Progress Toward Achieving Goals. Toward the end of the year, meet with your personnel to review the progress they have made toward achieving their goals. Form 2.8, Progress Appraisal Conference Form (see pages 80–82), is designed to facilitate that discussion. As you both reflect on the process during the year, be sure to recognize progress toward goals, even if those goals weren't fully achieved. Similar to the process you followed with Form 2.7, Goal-Setting Conference Form, you should fill out Form 2.8, but avoid dominating the discussion. The end of this conference should be an opportunity for discussing what has been helpful and what

might be done the next year to make the process even more valuable.

Personnel Evaluation Summary

Once you have finished evaluating personnel by using the tools you and your Coaching Committee decided on, take a few moments to complete Form 2.9, Personnel Evaluation Summary Form (see pages 83–85). This form is designed to assist you in assembling the results from the other forms for each of your personnel. As you complete this form, you will review the results of the other forms you have completed in evaluating personnel throughout the year and obtain a summary of your staff's strengths and weaknesses, which you can use in enhancing your program next year.

SUMMARY

You have now worked with your Coaching Committee to determine the minimum competencies for your coaches, and conducted conferences that have helped your coaches and other athletic program personnel to become more intrinsically motivated while they have pursued professional growth and development. You have taken important steps toward building a team of personnel who work together to support the program philosophy you began to develop in Part One. The last leg of your journey through program evaluation takes you inside your facilities, equipment, and program offerings. So keep your philosophy handy and move along to Part Three, where you will complete the evaluation of your athletic program.

*P*art *T*hree

Facility, Equipment, and Program Evaluation

In addition to evaluating personnel, your role as sport director carries responsibility for evaluating facilities, equipment, and the range of program offerings. Part Three of this guide provides you with tools to carry out these aspects of program evaluation.

FACILITIES AND EQUIPMENT

The key to keeping track of equipment and verifying that facilities are in good condition is delegating responsibility appropriately and developing good communication systems. This guide contains specialized tools designed to assist you in accomplishing five important goals:

- To ensure safety
- To ensure sufficient space for practices, contests, and storage
- To ensure sufficient equipment quantities
- To monitor efficiency of record-keeping systems
- To ensure cost effectiveness

This book cannot provide a comprehensive guide to facility and equipment management, an undertaking more appropriately presented in a separate book ASEP is currently developing as part of its SportDirector Series. But you will find a method, as you did in Part Two, for collecting information from multiple sources and using specific tools to collect that information efficiently and systematically. Table 3.1 (see page 34) depicts an overview of the facility and equipment evaluation tools discussed in Part Three.

Involving Your Coaching Committee

Before you begin your facility and equipment evaluation, bring together your Coaching Committee (see discussion on developing a Coaching Committee on page 16). Determine the most effective and efficient means for providing every facility and piece of equipment sufficient attention and inspection. In addition, discuss how decisions regarding the maintenance, upkeep, rental, and purchase of equipment and facilities will be made with attention to the organization's philosophy statement. For example, if your philosophy promotes skill development and physical fitness ahead of winning, you may need to look closely to verify that the budget reflects that priority. Special purchases that reward interscholastic varsity teams with the most wins may be appropriate, but they may not support your philosophy statement. And if these purchases coincide with

Table 3.1   Facility and Equipment Evaluation Tools

Goals	Data source	Collection tools
• Safety assurance • Sufficient space • Sufficient quantity	Sport directors	Form 3.1—Facilities Inspection Checklist
	Coaches and trainers	Form 3.2—Equipment Inspection Checklist
• Efficient system of record keeping	Sport directors	Form 3.3—Record-Keeping Checklist
• Cost effectiveness	Sport directors	Form 3.4—Facility Analysis Form Form 3.5—Equipment Analysis Form
	Coaches and trainers	Form 3.6—Facility and Equipment Questionnaire
• All goals	Sport directors	Form 3.7—Facility and Equipment Evaluation Summary Form

reductions in programs that appeal to large numbers of recreational sport participants, you may attract criticism from those whose programs have been cut. If your philosophy statement is to be meaningful, it must be reflected in budgetary decisions as well as on posters and season schedules.

Inspecting Facilities and Equipment

To ensure safety, sufficient space, and sufficient quantities of equipment, you need to conduct regular inspections. Take a moment to look over Form 3.1, Facilities Inspection Checklist, and Form 3.2, Equipment Inspection Checklist (see pages 86–93). Because the ultimate responsibility for facility safety lies with you as sport director, you should take the time to inspect each of your facilities carefully. Form 3.1 is a sample checklist that you might use to develop a more appropriate form for your facilities. As you develop your own version, consider developing separate sheets for each facility that you can distribute to the head coaches of each of your programs. Similarly, Form 3.2 is an incomplete checklist to help you develop a more appropriate form for your equipment. Again, by developing a separate sheet for each of your programs, you can involve coaches in the inspection process. Follow the guidelines you have established with the input of your Coaching Committee to determine who should conduct each inspection and the frequency of these inspections.

Developing Efficient Systems for Keeping Records

If you hope to keep up with your facility and equipment needs, you need to take some time to gather a number of records. Particularly if your organization delegates facility and equipment responsibilities to many different individuals, you may find the task of assembling all the information necessary to make good decisions a burden. By using Form 3.3, Record-Keeping Checklist (see page 94), you can reduce the anxiety that may arise over where to find important information, as well as implement a system for coordinating all the individuals who are responsible for handling records.

Begin by making a copy of Form 3.3, Record-Keeping Checklist, for each sport or program in your organization. Then, fill in the top section of the form to identify coaches and trainers with responsibility for that program. The rest of the form provides a listing of the specific types of records which these individuals may have responsibility for collecting. These records have been divided into the general categories of status reports, maintenance records, planning records, and other records. Customize these categories to fit your program needs.

Next, identify the dates by which each type of record should be given to you or your designee. Distribute copies of these forms to the head coach of each of your programs and make sure they are aware of their responsibilities for gathering these records. Establish a file system which follows the categories you have developed for your version of Form 3.3, Record-Keeping Checklist, and use one file folder to hold your copies of these checklists. By updating Form 3.3 and filing these records as they are turned in, you may quickly and easily check the status of all relevant facility and equipment records for you programs. If a form appears to be missing, you will be able to identify who has responsibility for providing it. And by taking a few minutes each week to check the dates when records are due, you can follow up with each of your program's head coaches, reducing the likelihood that important records disappear.

Analyzing Facility and Equipment Needs

Once you have collected all important records, you are ready to analyze your facility and equipment needs. Gather the records from your files, then turn to Form 3.4, Facility Analysis Form (see pages 95–97). Make a copy of Form 3.4 for each of your facilities. Start by filling in the facility name, then identify all the uses that are made of that facility.

Next, fill in the information in the accommodations section. Indicate the number of athletes and/ or teams which can use the facility simultaneously, as well as the spectator capacity. Complete this section by circling "yes" or "no" to indicate whether the facility contains accommodations for concessions, restrooms, lockers, storage, and media space. Two additional spaces are provided for identifying features of your facilities that do not appear on this form. Use the "comments" section to note any important information about each of these accommodations. For example, you may be filling out the

form for a gymnasium. While you circle "yes" to indicate that concessions are accommodated, you might use the comments line to note that you have been using a rented popcorn cart or that you have had difficulty providing enough space for patrons who are waiting for concessions.

The expenses section provides space for you to include estimates of expenses paid out in rent, utilities, maintenance, operation, and other categories. Once you have responded to these items, total your monthly and annual expenses and write these figures in the blanks at the bottom of the form.

The last section of Form 3.4 is designed to help you determine when your facility is in low and high demand. Fill in the boxes below each month with the names and dates when sports, programs, and special events rely on this facility. Then, complete the form by including any other comments that you feel are important to keep in mind but aren't covered by categories on this form.

Once you have completed Form 3.4 for each of your facilities, you will not only have a quick way to determine the range of demands on facilities but also to identify the costs of maintaining these facilities compared with that demand. This analysis can help you determine, for example, whether it would be cost effective to renovate a facility with little current use or in disrepair rather than continuing to rent an existing one. Also use this form to determine potential improvements in accommodations that might be justified based on expenses and frequency of use. And of course, compare these forms to identify which of your facilities represent the most and least efficient use of your organization's resources. If the second page of Form 3.4 shows that one of your facilities receives little use, check the accommodations to determine whether that lack of use might be related to inadequate storage or locker space. Check expenses to determine whether you should continue to use the facility or whether another use would be more appropriate.

Now it's time to work with Form 3.5, Equipment Analysis Form (see pages 98–100), to accomplish the same goals for equipment that you pursued for facilities using Form 3.4. This time, however, consider asking the head coach for each of your programs to fill out the form and return it to you. Usually, these coaches are in a much better position to know how much equipment they have and what condition that equipment is in. By gathering these forms for each of your programs, you will be able to compare their needs and make good decisions about how best to allocate limited financial resources.

If you are asking your coaches to complete Form 3.5 be sure that they understand in advance how to complete it properly. Otherwise, you may find a number of details that you need to follow up once you receive the forms back. Begin completing Form 3.5 by writing the name of the sport or program on the line at the top of the form. Next, look over the three sections under "Equipment status." Use Section I to list items in good condition, Section II for items in poor condition, and Section III for new items that need to be purchased. Each of these three areas asks for different information, so let's look at each individually.

For Section I of Form 3.5, use the lines at the left, under the heading "Description/date purchased," to write a brief description of all equipment and uniforms in good condition. Although you may wish to discuss with your coaches or your Coaching Committee the best criteria for determining whether equipment is in good condition, a general guideline might be to include in Part I any equipment that is likely to be useful not only for this year, but next year as well. That way, the only equipment listed in Part I that should impact the equipment budget is that which is damaged, lost, or stolen during the year. Use a separate line for each piece of equipment and uniforms to provide a more complete picture of the items in good condition. If you are looking at basketball uniforms, for example, you might use a separate line for practice jerseys,

game jerseys, and game shorts. You might also use separate lines for each color or style of each of these uniform elements. The more detailed your descriptions are, the easier it will be to make sound decisions about equipment needs.

After you have listed all items in good condition in Part I of Form 3.5, use the same line to identify as accurately as possible the date when each item was originally purchased (you may find another opportunity here for involving support staff in your evaluation by asking them to look up records of these purchases). Complete Part I by listing the quantity of each of these items that is in good condition.

To fill out the "Description/date purchased" and "Quantity" columns of Part II of Form 3.5, use a process similar to that used in Part I. Part II, though, is used to list items in poor condition. Once again, you may wish to consult with coaches or your Coaching Committee to discuss the criteria that will be used to determine what constitutes poor condition. The form has been set up, though, so that any equipment not listed in Part I will appear in Part II. Items in Part II may still have a season left in them, but that determination needs to be made based on the potential safety risk for athletes using the equipment, as well as the constraints of the equipment budget. To help you determine whether to repair or replace these items, you or someone you designate—like a coach or member of your support staff—need to determine the costs for repairing and replacing these items.

You have a couple of options for completing the "Recommendation/cost" portion of Part II of Form 3.5, Equipment Analysis Form. If you ask

your head coaches to complete the form, you might also ask them to recommend whether to repair or replace specific equipment. You would then decide whether to accept or reject their recommendations as part of your equipment budgeting process. An advantage to this approach is that it provides coaches the opportunity to identify which items they would prefer to have replaced rather than repaired. As long as the coaches recognize that their recommendations will be considered, but might need to be altered due to budget constraints, this approach tends to promote good relations between you and your coaching staff. Of course, you still might choose to ask coaches to leave this space blank, in which case you would complete it as you look into the equipment budget and the needs of all your program offerings. Either way, it's important that you make decisions about repairing and replacing equipment based on specific quotes of costs, either from current equipment catalogs or by quotes from sales representatives. Finally, once you have decided on whether to repair or replace all equipment listed in Part II, use the box at the bottom of Part II to write the "Total cost" of all equipment repair and replacement.

Complete Part III of Form 3.5 by listing descriptions, quantity, and costs of new equipment that needs to be purchased but is not listed in Part II. These expenses might range from small disposable items, such as first aid equipment, to large items, such as a pole vault pit. As you did in Part II, obtain accurate quotes of costs and report the "Total cost" at the bottom of the form. You will be able to use the results of this part of the form to compare needs for new equipment purchases for each of your program offerings and make sound judgments about how to allocate equipment budgets.

At the end of Form 3.5 is a place for you and/or the coaches who helped complete the form to write any additional comments that are important to consider when analyzing equipment needs for the coming year. Be sure to use this space for important considerations that you don't want to forget!

Now you are ready to use Form 3.6, Facilities and Equipment Questionnaire (see pages 101–102), to collect additional information about the needs of your programs. Distribute this form to all your coaches and trainers, then collect and review the results to determine whether your coaches and trainers have concerns about their facilities and equip-

ment. Be sure to save yourself time by completing the top portion of the form before making the copies! To encourage these individuals to take the form seriously, you should follow up in a timely manner on areas of concern. If coaches and trainers feel that their feedback may have been overlooked, they will be less likely to provide you with the information you need to maintain the quality of your athletic program's equipment and facilities.

Now that you have collected information on facility and equipment needs, use Form 3.7, Facility and Equipment Evaluation Summary Form (see pages 103–104), to summarize your comments. Notice that each page of the form has been designed to be duplicated as many times as necessary to provide sufficient space for all of your facilities and equipment. Use this form to create a summary of your facility and equipment needs as you prepare your budget for the coming year. This form will become especially valuable when prioritizing budget requests due to fiscal limitations.

PROGRAM OFFERINGS

In addition to evaluating your personnel, facilities, and equipment, you need to take one more step to complete your evaluation. This final step is to evaluate your program offerings. Part Three of this guide discusses tools designed to assist you in achieving four program evaluation goals:

- To ensure safety
- To ensure cost effectiveness
- To ensure sufficient breadth of programs
- To ensure acceptable levels of access to programs

Table 3.2 provides an overview of the program evaluation tools in this guide.

Before plunging into your program evaluation, you should take a moment to reflect upon the implications of two important pieces of federal legislation. The first is Title IX of the Education Amendments of 1972. Title IX was established to protect individuals' rights and prohibited gender-based discrimination in educational programs receiving federal funding. Specifically, Title IX states

Table 3.2   Program Evaluation Tools

Goals	Data source	Collection tools
• Safety assurance • Cost effectiveness	Sport directors	Form 3.8—Sport Director's Program Identification Form
• Sufficient breadth • Acceptable access	Coaches and trainers Athletes Parents	Form 3.9—Sport Program Questionnaire
• All goals	Sport directors	Form 3.10—Program Analysis Summary Form

No person in the United States shall, on the basis of sex, be excluded from participating in, be denied the benefits of, or be subjected to discrimination under any education program or activity receiving Federal financial assistance . . . .

If you are the sport director of an organization receiving federal financial assistance, and you fail to provide appropriate access to programs for females, you may be in violation of Title IX, and you may lose your federal funding.

The second important piece of legislation you should consider is known as the Americans with Disabilities Act (ADA), which extends the protection of the 1964 Civil Rights Act to individuals with disabilities. The ADA states

No individuals shall be discriminated against on the basis of disabilities in the full and equal enjoyment of goods, services, facilities, privileges, advantages or accommodations at any place of public accommodation by any person who owns, leases or operates a place of public accommodation.

Benefits provided for the disabled cannot be separate or different from those provided for others, unless they are as effective as those provided for others.

While it is still somewhat difficult to determine exactly how the ADA will affect athletic programs, it is essential that you recognize that the law has been established to provide individuals with disabilities the same opportunities for involvement afforded to those without disabilities.

To discuss in detail how these laws affect your decisions in offering programs is beyond the intent of this guide. However, you are encouraged to make your Coaching Committee aware of these laws and to obtain more information about how these laws might affect your programs. Contact either your state athletic association, the United States Olympic Committee, or the United States Department of Justice for further information.

U.S. Olympic Committee
Department of Disabled Sports Services
One Olympic Plaza
Colorado Springs, CO 80909-5760
(719) 578-4680

U.S. Department of Justice
Civil Rights Division
Coordination and Review Section
P.O. Box 66118
Washington, DC 20035-6118
(202) 514-0301

Identifying Program Status

Before you can determine whether programs need to be added, modified, or cut, you must first determine how many programs you currently offer, as well as identify the number and composition of the athletes in those programs. Form 3.8, Sport Director's Program Identification Form (see pages 105–107), asks you to indicate which programs you offer as interscholastic sports, club sports, intramural sports, or other programs. For each program offering, circle the gender descriptors necessary to indicate whether programs exist only for males, only for females, for both males and females (circle both), or as coed programs. Next, indicate the number of individuals who participated in these programs last year and this year. When you have completed the form, you will have compiled a convenient summary of the breadth of your athletic program offerings, and you will be able to make some initial determinations regarding which programs appear to have the greatest appeal.

Obtaining Input

The next step in evaluating your program offerings is to distribute, collect, and analyze the results of Form 3.9, Sport Program Questionnaire (see pages 108–109). Although you might use this form as is, you are encouraged to involve your Coaching Committee in determining the precise items to include on your questionnaire. It is important to ask questions that will assist you in determining whether your program offerings appeal to all prospective athletes in your organization. To collect enough input to guide your decision-making, distribute this form to the widest possible range of individuals, including athletes, parents, coaches, trainers, and other staff members. Refer to the description in Part Two of distributing, collecting, and analyzing the results of questionnaires to assist you in carrying out this portion of the evaluation (see pages 25–28).

Analyzing Program Offerings

Your next step should be to complete Form 3.10, Program Analysis Summary Form (see pages 110–113). Use Part I of the form to summarize the results you obtained from Form 3.9, Sport Program Questionnaire. You can see that the concerns from these questionnaires have been divided into areas of quality and safety, depth and breadth, and access. These categories will help you to determine what concerns are most important in relation to your program offerings as a whole. Compare these results to those you obtained on Form 3.8, Sport Director's Program Identification Form (see pages 105–107), to determine whether depth and breadth and access concerns are also reflected in the numbers and composition of athletes who participate in your program offerings.

Next, use Part II of Form 3.10, Program Analysis Summary Form, to summarize the expenses and income generated by each of your programs. Although it may take some time to collect all of this information, it is essential that you have a clear understanding of the costs of your programs to help you make sound recommendations for changes. The following example shows how important this information can be.

Paulette is a high school athletic director facing the difficult decision of having to cut $10,000.00 from her school's athletic program budget. She has been instructed to achieve this cut through the elimination of interscholastic programs. No matter which programs she chooses, a number of people are going to be angry, so she knows that she has to do the best job possible. Figure 3.1 depicts Part II of Paulette's Form 3.10. Which do you suppose she should eliminate?

Although some might say that the football program brings in the most money ($8,696.00) and should therefore be spared, even with that revenue the football program actually costs Paulette's school $9,569.00! In contrast, although a sport like softball might not bring in any revenue, it only costs the school $3,838.00 to operate. If the numbers of participants for softball and football are roughly the same, should Paulette elect to eliminate the football program? Obviously, there are a number of other issues to take into account besides the budget. Still, this example demonstrates how your perception of the costs of offering a sport program might differ from the actual figures. Part II of Form 3.10 may not provide you with easy answers, but it can help you avoid making decisions based on faulty assumptions.

Figure 3.1   Paulette's program cost analysis.

II. Program cost analysis

Sport	Expenses					Income		Net expense income
	Salary	Facility	Equipment	Transport	Other (Dues)	Fees	Receipts	
football	$9,113	$4,970	$2,800	$1,332	$ 50	—	$8,696	$–9,569
b basketball	6,878	2,655	500	2,495	80	—	6,681	–5,927
wrestling	4,453	1,135	500	2,343	375	—	778	–8,028
b track	2,835	100	500	1,073	340	—	—	–4,848
cross-country	3,142	300	350	1,925	450	—	—	–6,167
volleyball	6,362	1,065	500	1,611	150	—	1,764	–7,924
g basketball	4,867	1,730	500	2,552	150	—	2,482	–7,317
g track	3,211	380	500	1,555	340	—	—	–5,986
softball	1,510	880	500	898	50	—	—	–3,838
baseball	2,002	880	500	1,465	50	—	—	–4,897
cheerleading	1,510	—	300	—	—	—	—	–1,810
Totals	$45,883	$14,095	$7,450	$17,249	$2,035	—	$20,401	$–66,311

Use Part III of this form to record your concerns and recommendations for program offerings. As you complete Part III, remain conscious of your philosophy statement. When tough decisions have to be made, let your philosophy suggest the best direction for movement.

Pursuing Program Changes

Finally, you will need to work with your administration and Coaching Committee to plan and implement changes in your program offerings. Use Form 3.10, Program Analysis Summary Form, to make your presentation to these individuals and groups, then work with them to implement changes. Recognize that you will never be able to please every individual and that small groups of people will always criticize. But if you have let your philosophy stand as the foundation on which your decisions have been built, your integrity should remain above reproach.

SUMMARY

Now that you have completed this cycle of program evaluation, you can look back with satisfaction upon the careful way you have gone about evaluating the safety and efficiency of your facilities and equipment. You can also speak more confidently of how your athletic program offerings meet the needs of your athletes, coaches, trainers, parents, and other members of your athletic program and the community beyond. But before you close the cover, you also recognize that effective program evaluation is an on-going process. This year, and every year, can serve to strengthen your commitment and that of your organization to the philosophy behind your athletic program. So take a few moments to relax and reflect on the work that you and your athletic program personnel have accomplished. Put your tools away for now, but don't let them get too dusty. You'll be coming back to them again soon to make next year's program even better for your athletes and more manageable for you!

 **Form 1.1**

IDENTIFYING EVALUATION NEEDS

Use this form to identify the range of program elements and personnel to be evaluated. With this information you will be better able to establish a plan for conducting an effective program evaluation. Prepare one copy of this form for each interscholastic, club, intramural, and other sport program offering.

I. General description

Fill in the blanks on the first line below to indicate the type of sport and gender of participants. On the next line, identify whether the sport is interscholastic, club, intramural, or some other program offering. If you circle "other," write the type of program offering on the line. Finally, on the third line indicate the start and end dates of the season, from the opening date of practices to the final date of championships or tournaments.

Sport: _____   Gender (circle):   male   female   coed

Type of program offering (circle):   interscholastic   club   intramural   other _____

Season starts: _____   Season ends: _____

II. Personnel

Use the spaces below to list the names of coaches, trainers, and other personnel with responsibility for conducting this program offering.

Head coach: _____

Assistant coach: _____

Assistant coach: _____

Athletic trainer: _____

Other: _____

Other: _____

Immediate supervisor for above personnel: _____

III. Facilities

Use the spaces below to provide the name and/or location of each facility used for this program offering.

Primary practice facility: _____

Secondary practice facility: _____

Other practice facility: _____

Contest facility: _____

Primary equipment storage facility: _____

Secondary equipment storage facility: _____

IV. Equipment

Fill out the following table to list all uniforms, as well as safety, practice, and contest equipment. Indicate the quantity currently on hand and where each item is currently stored.

Item	Quantity on hand	Storage facility
_____	_____	_____
_____	_____	_____
_____	_____	_____
_____	_____	_____
_____	_____	_____
_____	_____	_____
_____	_____	_____
_____	_____	_____
_____	_____	_____
_____	_____	_____
_____	_____	_____
_____	_____	_____
_____	_____	_____

Form 2.1

SUMMATIVE COACH EVALUATION INSTRUMENT

Coach:_____   Position: _____   Date:_____

Observer:_____   Location and activity: _____

Goals:	Safety assurance
	Duty proficiency
	Administrative competence

This form helps you determine whether coaches meet established minimum standards of performance in the areas of safety, duty proficiency, and administrative competence. Each of these areas is covered by a separate part of this form. Parts I and II should be completed by direct observation of a coach's practice(s) and/or contest(s), while Part III should be completed by collecting appropriate documents.

To complete the form, circle the response that best describes the coach's performance for each descriptor. If the answer is difficult to determine, or cannot be determined at this time, circle the question mark. In the space below each descriptor, labeled "Observations," write a brief description of the specific performance that led to your response.

Part I: Safety assurance (collect via observation)

1. Removes hazards from practice/contest area	yes	no	?
Observations:			
2. Inspects equipment for hazards	yes	no	?
Observations:			
3. Removes hazardous equipment	yes	no	?
Observations:			
4. Adapts to environmental/weather hazards appropriately	yes	no	?
Observations:			
5. Warns athletes of inherent risks of activities	yes	no	?
Observations:			

6. Provides warm up before more intense activity	yes	no	?
Observations:			

7. Provides stretching before practice/contest	yes	no	?
Observations:			

8. Adapts activities for participation of those physically challenged	yes	no	?
Observations:			

9. Supervises all athletes appropriately	yes	no	?
Observations:			

10. Corrects athletes exhibiting hazardous behaviors	yes	no	?
Observations:			

11. Matches athletes by skill level	yes	no	?
Observations:			

12. Matches athletes by size	yes	no	?
Observations:			

13. Adjusts practices/contests to skill/interest level of athletes	yes	no	?
Observations:			

14. Develops adequate conditioning for physical fitness in athletes	yes	no	?
Observations:			

15. Conducts practices using safe skill progression	yes	no	?
Observations:			

16. Provides adequate water breaks	yes	no	?
Observations:			

17. Attends to injured athletes quickly	yes	no	?
Observations:			

18. Attends to injured athletes appropriately	yes	no	?
Observations:			

19. Provides cool down after intense activity	yes	no	?
Observations.			

20. Provides stretching after practice/contest	yes	no	?
Observations:			

21. Appropriately supervises athletes not actively involved in practice/contest (injured, ineligible, etc.)	yes	no	?
Observations:			

22. Follows recommendations of trainers/physicians	yes	no	?
Observations:			

23. Meets other responsibilities for safety (list)	yes	no	?
Observations:			

24. Meets other responsibilities for safety (list)	yes	no	?
Observations:			

25. Meets other responsibilities for safety (list)	yes	no	?
Observations:			

Part II: Duty proficiency (collect via observation)

1. Starts practice/contest on time	yes	no	?
Observations:			

2. Arranges athletes so all can see/hear instruction	yes	no	?
Observations:			

3. Gains athletes' attention before speaking	yes	no	?
Observations:			

4. Displays enthusiasm	yes	no	?
Observations:			

5. Introduces skill/drill/strategy	yes	no	?
Observations:			

6. Demonstrates skill/drill/strategy effectively	yes	no	?
Observations:			

7. Demonstrates from different angles	yes	no	?
Observations:			

8. Repeats demonstrations	yes	no	?
Observations:			

9. Explains purpose(s) of skill/drill/strategy	yes	no	?
Observations:			

10. Provides clear instruction	yes	no	?
Observations:			

11. Attends to athletes as they practice	yes	no	?
Observations:			

12. Provides positive feedback to athletes	yes	no	?
Observations:			

13. Avoids criticizing athletes	yes	no	?
Observations:			

14. Corrects athletes' mistakes in humane manner	yes	no	?
Observations:			

15. Involves all athletes in constructive activity	yes	no	?
Observations:			

16. Follows practice plan	yes	no	?
Observations:			

17. Uses practice time effectively	yes	no	?
Observations:			

18. Uses appropriate language in practices/contests	yes	no	?
Observations:			

19. Interacts with athletes in professional manner	yes	no	?
Observations:			

20. Provides athletes feedback on progress	yes	no	?
Observations:			

21. Provides opportunities for all athletes to succeed	yes	no	?
Observations:			

22. Provides consequences for negative behavior	yes	no	?
Observations:			

23. Provides variety of approaches/activities for skills/drills	yes	no	?
Observations:			

24. Encourages commitment and pride in athletes	yes	no	?
Observations:			

25. Maintains poise in unexpected situations	yes	no	?
Observations:			

26. Reviews athletes' and team's progress	yes	no	?
Observations:			

27. Demonstrates adequate knowledge of sport	yes	no	?
Observations:			

28. Demonstrates understanding of effective strategy in contests/practices	yes	no	?
Observations:			

29. Delegates responsibilities appropriately	yes	no	?
Observations:			

30. Provides opportunities for athletes to develop leadership	yes	no	?
Observations:			

31. Manages conflict effectively	yes	no	?
Observations:			

32. Provides opportunities for athletes' questions	yes	no	?
Observations:			

33. Responds to athletes' questions professionally	yes	no	?
Observations:			

34. Follows through with promises	yes	no	?
Observations:			

35. Ends practice/contest on time	yes	no	?
Observations:			

36. Promotes academic success	yes	no	?
Observations:			

37. Enforces school/organization policies consistently	yes	no	?
Observations:			

38. Interacts with administrators in professional manner	yes	no	?
Observations:			

39. Interacts with colleagues in professional manner	yes	no	?
Observations:			

40. Interacts with media in professional manner	yes	no	?
Observations:			

41. Interacts with officials in professional manner	yes	no	?
Observations:			

42. Interacts with parents in professional manner	yes	no	?
Observations:			

43. Models appropriate behavior	yes	no	?
Observations:			

44. Performs other duties appropriately (list)	yes	no	?
Observations:			

45. Performs other duties appropriately (list)	yes	no	?
Observations:			

46. Performs other duties appropriately (list)	yes	no	?
Observations:			

Part III: Administrative competence (obtain via document collection)

1. Attends required district meetings	yes	no	?
Documentation:			
2. Attends rules meetings	yes	no	?
Documentation:			
3. Submits athlete physicals on time	yes	no	?
Documentation:			
4. Submits athlete waivers on time	yes	no	?
Documentation:			
5. Submits equipment inventories on time	yes	no	?
Documentation:			
6. Submits budgets on time	yes	no	?
Documentation:			
7. Informs athletes of insurance policies available through district/organization	yes	no	?
Documentation:			
8. Conducts preseason meetings with athletes	yes	no	?
Documentation:			
9. Conducts preseason meetings with parents	yes	no	?
Documentation:			

10. Establishes realistic goals for athletes, team, staff, and self	yes	no	?
Documentation:			

11. Establishes performance goals over outcome goals	yes	no	?
Documentation:			

12. Keeps attendance records	yes	no	?
Documentation:			

13. Monitors athletes' academic progress	yes	no	?
Documentation:			

14. Conducts effective meetings	yes	no	?
Documentation:			

15. Keeps administrators appropriately informed	yes	no	?
Documentation:			

16. Takes responsibility for actions/words	yes	no	?
Documentation:			

17. Conducts practices/contests from clearly defined objectives	yes	no	?
Documentation:			

18. Conducts practices based on physiological principles of training and biomechanically safe skill progressions	yes	no	?
Documentation:			

19. Evaluates team personnel appropriately	yes	no	?
Documentation:			

20. Follows season plan	yes	no	?
Documentation:			

21. Supervises distribution of uniforms and equipment	yes	no	?
Documentation:			

22. Supervises collection of uniforms and equipment	yes	no	?
Documentation:			

23. Maintains records	yes	no	?
Documentation:			

24. Reports results of contests to media effectively	yes	no	?
Documentation:			

25. Meets other organizational responsibilities (list)	yes	no	?
Documentation:			

26. Meets other organizational responsibilities (list)	yes	no	?
Documentation:			

27. Meets other organizational responsibilities (list)	yes	no	?
Documentation:			

Form 2.2

COLLEAGUE QUESTIONNAIRE

Please return to: _____   Date distributed: _____

Please return by: _____

Because we believe it essential to work together for the positive development of our athletes, we are requesting that you take a few moments to provide feedback about the coaches whose names appear below. Please submit your comments anonymously. Although the form will not be shared with the coaches, the collective comments of all staff members will be used to assist them in identifying areas for professional growth. Thank you in advance for your time.

To complete the form, circle the response that best describes each coach's performance for each descriptor. If the answer is difficult to determine, or cannot be determined at this time, circle the question mark. In the space below each descriptor, labeled "Observations," write a brief description of the specific performance that led you to circle your response for each coach.

	Coach 1	Coach 2	Coach 3	Coach 4
1. Monitors athletes' academic progress	yes no ?	yes no ?	yes no ?	yes no ?
Observations				
Coach 1		Coach 2		
Coach 3		Coach 4		

	Coach 1	Coach 2	Coach 3	Coach 4
2. Solicits colleagues' input when appropriate	yes no ?	yes no ?	yes no ?	yes no ?

Observations	
Coach 1	Coach 2
Coach 3	Coach 4

	Coach 1	Coach 2	Coach 3	Coach 4
3. Communicates goals and expectations clearly	yes no ?	yes no ?	yes no ?	yes no ?

Observations	
Coach 1	Coach 2
Coach 3	Coach 4

4. Demonstrates enthusiasm	Coach 1	Coach 2	Coach 3	Coach 4	
	yes no ?	yes no ?	yes no ?	yes no ?	

Observations	
Coach 1	Coach 2
Coach 3	Coach 4

5. Demonstrates genuine interest in athletes' well-being	Coach 1	Coach 2	Coach 3	Coach 4	
	yes no ?	yes no ?	yes no ?	yes no ?	

Observations	
Coach 1	Coach 2
Coach 3	Coach 4

	Coach 1	Coach 2	Coach 3	Coach 4
6. Provides equal opportunities for all athletes to succeed	yes no ?	yes no ?	yes no ?	yes no ?

Observations	
Coach 1	Coach 2
Coach 3	Coach 4

	Coach 1	Coach 2	Coach 3	Coach 4
7. Emphasizes athletes' development over winning	yes no ?	yes no ?	yes no ?	yes no ?

Observations	
Coach 1	Coach 2
Coach 3	Coach 4

	Coach 1	Coach 2	Coach 3	Coach 4	
8. Demonstrates self-control	yes no ?	yes no ?	yes no ?	yes no ?	

Observations	
Coach 1	Coach 2
Coach 3	Coach 4

	Coach 1	Coach 2	Coach 3	Coach 4	
9. Models principles of good sport conduct	yes no ?	yes no ?	yes no ?	yes no ?	

Observations	
Coach 1	Coach 2
Coach 3	Coach 4

	Coach 1	Coach 2	Coach 3	Coach 4
10. Considers special circumstances when applying policies	yes no ?	yes no ?	yes no ?	yes no ?

Observations	
Coach 1	Coach 2
Coach 3	Coach 4

	Coach 1	Coach 2	Coach 3	Coach 4
11. Enforces policies consistently	yes no ?	yes no ?	yes no ?	yes no ?

Observations	
Coach 1	Coach 2
Coach 3	Coach 4

	Coach 1	Coach 2	Coach 3	Coach 4
12. Emphasizes importance of athletes' academic pursuits	yes no ?	yes no ?	yes no ?	yes no ?

Observations	
Coach 1	Coach 2
Coach 3	Coach 4

	Coach 1	Coach 2	Coach 3	Coach 4
13. Provides adequate notice when requesting schedule changes	yes no ?	yes no ?	yes no ?	yes no ?

Observations	
Coach 1	Coach 2
Coach 3	Coach 4

	Coach 1	Coach 2	Coach 3	Coach 4
14. Provides athletes with rewarding sport experiences	yes no ?	yes no ?	yes no ?	yes no ?

Observations	
Coach 1	Coach 2
Coach 3	Coach 4

	Coach 1	Coach 2	Coach 3	Coach 4
15. Attends to athletes who disrupt practices/contests	yes no ?	yes no ?	yes no ?	yes no ?

Observations	
Coach 1	Coach 2
Coach 3	Coach 4

	Coach 1	Coach 2	Coach 3	Coach 4
16. Motivates athletes to improve their sport skills and physical fitness	yes no ?	yes no ?	yes no ?	yes no ?

Observations	
Coach 1	Coach 2
Coach 3	Coach 4

	Coach 1	Coach 2	Coach 3	Coach 4
17. Develops athletes' leadership skills	yes no ?	yes no ?	yes no ?	yes no ?

Observations	
Coach 1	Coach 2
Coach 3	Coach 4

	Coach 1	Coach 2	Coach 3	Coach 4
18. Emphasizes safety during practices and contests	yes no ?	yes no ?	yes no ?	yes no ?

Observations	
Coach 1	Coach 2
Coach 3	Coach 4

	Coach 1	Coach 2	Coach 3	Coach 4
19. Appears well organized	yes no ?	yes no ?	yes no ?	yes no ?

Observations	
Coach 1	Coach 2
Coach 3	Coach 4

	Coach 1	Coach 2	Coach 3	Coach 4
20. Provides colleagues with opportunities for involvement	yes no ?	yes no ?	yes no ?	yes no ?

Observations	
Coach 1	Coach 2
Coach 3	Coach 4

Use the space below to provide additional feedback that might promote the professional development of the coaches.

Thank you for your time!

 **Form 2.3**

ATHLETE QUESTIONNAIRE

Coach: _____   Date distributed: _____

Please return to: _____   **Please return by:** _____

We are requesting that you take a few moments to provide feedback about your coach, whose name appears above. Please submit your comments anonymously. Although the form will not be shared with the coach, the collective comments of all athletes on the team will be used to assist the coach in identifying areas for professional growth. Thank you in advance for your time.

To complete the form, circle the response that best describes the coach's performance for each descriptor. If the answer is difficult to determine, or cannot be determined at this time, circle the question mark. In the space below each descriptor, labeled "Observations," write a brief description of the specific performance that led you to circle your response.

1. My coach talks to me when my grades are low.	yes	no	?
Observations:			
2. I feel comfortable approaching my coach with a question or idea.	yes	no	?
Observations:			
3. I know what my coach's goals for the season are.	yes	no	?
Observations:			
4. My coach is enthusiastic.	yes	no	?
Observations:			
5. My coach helps me set and achieve personal goals for the season.	yes	no	?
Observations:			
6. My coach provides equal opportunities for all athletes to succeed.	yes	no	?
Observations:			

7. My coach focuses more on skill improvement than on winning.	yes	no	?
Observations:			
8. My coach maintains self control.	yes	no	?
Observations:			
9. My coach models principles of good sport conduct.	yes	no	?
Observations:			
10. My coach considers special circumstances when applying policies.	yes	no	?
Observations:			
11. My coach enforces policies consistently.	yes	no	?
Observations:			
12. My coach encourages me to develop my academic skills.	yes	no	?
Observations:			
13. My coach provides adequate notice when making schedule changes.	yes	no	?
Observations:			
14. My coach makes participating in this sport a rewarding experience.	yes	no	?
Observations:			
15. My coach attends to athletes who disrupt practices.	yes	no	?
Observations:			
16. My coach helps me feel motivated to improve my sport skills and physical fitness.	yes	no	?
Observations:			

17. My coach provides me with opportunities to take a leadership role.	yes	no	?
Observations:			

18. My coach emphasizes safety during practices and contests.	yes	no	?
Observations:			

19. My coach appears well organized.	yes	no	?
Observations:			

20. I have improved my skills during this season.	yes	no	?
Observations:			

21. My coach provides individual attention to athletes who are having trouble.	yes	no	?
Observations:			

22. My coach seems to know a lot about this sport.	yes	no	?
Observations:			

Use the space below to provide additional feedback that might help your coach improve.

Thank you for your time!

Form 2.4

PARENT QUESTIONNAIRE

Coach: _____   Date distributed: _____

Please return to: _____   **Please return by:** _____

We are requesting that you take a few moments to provide feedback about your child's coach, whose name appears above. Please submit your comments anonymously. Although the form will not be shared with the coach, the collective comments of all athletes' parents will be used to assist the coach in identifying areas for professional growth. Thank you in advance for your time.

To complete the form, circle the response that best describes the coach's performance for each descriptor. If the answer is difficult to determine, or cannot be determined at this time, circle the question mark. In the space below each descriptor, labeled "Observations," write a brief description of the specific performance that led you to circle your response.

1. The coach monitors my child's grades.	yes	no	?
Observations:			

2. I feel comfortable approaching my child's coach with a question or idea.	yes	no	?
Observations:			

3. I know what the coach's goals for the season are.	yes	no	?
Observations:			

4. My child's coach is enthusiastic.	yes	no	?
Observations:			

5. The coach helps my child set and achieve personal goals for the season.	yes	no	?
Observations:			

6. My child's coach provides equal opportunities for all athletes to succeed.	yes	no	?
Observations:			

7. The coach focuses more on skill improvement than on winning.	yes	no	?
Observations:			

8. My child's coach maintains self control.	yes	no	?
Observations:			

9. The coach models principles of good sport conduct.	yes	no	?
Observations:			

10. My child's coach considers special circumstances when applying policies.	yes	no	?
Observations:			

11. The coach enforces policies consistently.	yes	no	?
Observations:			

12. The coach encourages my child to develop academic skills.	yes	no	?
Observations:			

13. The coach provides adequate notice when making schedule changes.	yes	no	?
Observations:			

14. My child finds participating in this sport a rewarding experience.	yes	no	?
Observations:			

15. The coach attends to athletes who disrupt practices.	yes	no	?
Observations:			

16. The coach helps my child feel motivated to improve sport skills and physical fitness.	yes	no	?
Observations:			
17. The coach provides my child with opportunities to take a leadership role.	yes	no	?
Observations:			
18. The coach emphasizes safety during practices and contests.	yes	no	?
Observations:			
19. The coach appears well organized.	yes	no	?
Observations:			
20. My child has improved skills during this season.	yes	no	?
Observations:			
21. The coach provides individual attention to athletes who are having trouble.	yes	no	?
Observations:			
22. My child's coach seems to know a lot about this sport.	yes	no	?
Observations:			

Use the space below to provide additional feedback that might help your son's or daughter's coach improve.

Thank you for your time!

Form 2.5

COACH SELF-APPRAISAL FORM

Coach: _____   Date distributed: _____

Please return to: _____   **Please return by:** _____

We are requesting that you take a few moments to provide feedback about your coaching performance. To complete the form, circle the response that best describes your performance for each descriptor. If the answer is difficult to determine, or cannot be determined at this time, circle the question mark. In the space below each descriptor, labeled "Comments," write a brief description of the actions you took this season that led you to circle your response. Thank you in advance for your time.

1. I monitor athletes' academic progress.	yes	no	?
Comments:			
2. I encourage athletes, parents, colleagues, and administrators to approach me with questions or ideas.	yes	no	?
Comments:			
3. I clearly communicate my goals and expectations.	yes	no	?
Comments:			
4. I demonstrate enthusiasm.	yes	no	?
Comments:			
5. I help athletes set and achieve personal goals for the season.	yes	no	?
Comments:			
6. I provide equal opportunities for all athletes to succeed.	yes	no	?
Comments:			

7. I focus more on skill improvement than on winning.	yes	no	?
Comments:			
8. I maintain self control.	yes	no	?
Comments:			
9. I model principles of good sport conduct.	yes	no	?
Comments:			
10. I consider special circumstances when applying policies.	yes	no	?
Comments:			
11. I enforce policies consistently.	yes	no	?
Comments:			
12. I encourage athletes to develop their academic skills.	yes	no	?
Comments:			
13. I provide adequate notice when making schedule changes.	yes	no	?
Comments:			
14. I provide athletes with rewarding sport experiences.	yes	no	?
Comments:			
15. I attend to athletes who disrupt practices.	yes	no	?
Comments;			
16. I motivate athletes to improve their sport skills and physical fitness.	yes	no	?
Comments:			

17. I provide athletes with opportunities to take leadership roles.	yes	no	?
Comments:			

18. I emphasize safety during practices and contests.	yes	no	?
Comments:			

19. I am well organized.	yes	no	?
Comments:			

20. I provide colleagues and parents with opportunities for involvement.	yes	no	?
Comments:			

21. I provide individual attention to athletes who are having trouble.	yes	no	?
Comments:			

22. I know a lot about this sport.	yes	no	?
Comments:			

Use the space below to include additional questions or comments.

Thank you for your time!

 Form 2.6

GOAL IDENTIFICATION FORM

Name: _____   Date distributed: _____

Please return to: _____   **Please return by:** _____

You play a vital role in our athletic program's ability to develop athletes to their greatest potential. At the same time, we believe that our program should place you in a position that encourages and assists you in growing professionally. To ensure that we take the steps necessary to promote your professional growth, we would like you to answer the following questions, which will help you set goals for the coming year.

As you think about your goals, consider areas of your performance that you would like to strengthen, as well as areas you would like to learn more about. Once you have completed the form, we will meet to discuss your goals and how we can work together to reach them.

Step 1: Identify areas for professional growth.

List four areas of your professional responsibilities that you would like to improve during the course of the coming year. The following are sample responses that might be appropriate for coaches: motivating athletes, zone defense, parent involvement. Thinking about your own responsibilities, which areas would you like to improve?

1. _____
2. _____
3. _____
4. _____

Step 2: Identify specific goal statements.

Examine each of the areas you identified in Step 1, and use the space below to rephrase each of your responses in the form of a goal. The more specific you can make your goal statements now, the easier it will be able to judge your achievements. For example, if you had written "motivating athletes" on the first line in Step 1, you might write the following goal statement on the first line below: "to motivate athletes to give 100 % effort in every practice." What are your goals?

1. _____
2. _____
3. _____
4. _____

Step 3: Identify actions to take in pursuit of goals.

For each of the goals you have written in Step 2, list two specific actions you could take to reach your goals. Following the example given in Step 2, you might list these actions. Action 1: "Read a book about motivating athletes." Action 2: "Observe Coach Rodriguez's practices." What actions might you take to reach your goals?

First goal

Action 1: _____

Action 2: _____

Second goal

Action 1: _____

Action 2: _____

Third goal

Action 1: _____

Action 2: _____

Fourth goal

Action 1: _____

Action 2: _____

Step 4: Identify actions for administrator to take to assist pursuit of goals.

For each of the goals identified in Step 2, list two actions that your athletic administrator could take to assist you in reaching your goals. Again, following the example in Step 2, you might list these actions. Action 1: "Observe my practices and suggest techniques that would fit into my system." Action 2: "Identify coaches who are effective motivators and whom I might observe."

First goal

Action 1: _____

Action 2: _____

Second goal

Action 1: _____

Action 2: _____

Third goal

Action 1: _____

Action 2: _____

Fourth goal

Action 1: _____

Action 2: _____

 **Form 2.7**

GOAL-SETTING CONFERENCE FORM

Sport directors and personnel should use this form to facilitate discussion of the results of Form 2.6, Goal Identification Form. Although the sport director should take responsibility for filling in the items on this form, the sport director and the individual being evaluated should work together to determine the best responses for each step. Remember that the formative evaluation process is designed to assist personnel in achieving their own goals for professional growth and development. This form is designed to help the sport director and the individual being evaluated identify effective ways to achieve those goals.

Name: _____   Position: _____

Sport director: _____   Date: _____

Step 1: Prioritize goals.

Examine the four goals listed in Step 2 of Form 2.6, Goal Identification Form. Select two or three goals for the individual to strive to achieve during the coming year. Use the spaces below to write the specific goals in order of priority.

1. _____

2. _____

3. _____

Step 2: Identify action to take in pursuit of goals.

For each of the goals listed above, discuss the actions listed in Step 3 of Form 2.6, Goal Identification Form. Once you have agreed upon specific actions the individual will take to achieve each goal, write those actions in the spaces below.

First goal

Action 1: _____

Action 2: _____

Second goal

Action 1: _____

Action 2: _____

Third goal

Action 1: _____

Action 2: _____

Step 3: Identify actions for sport director to take to assist pursuit of goals.

For each of the goals you just listed in Step 2, discuss the actions listed in Step 4 of Form 2.6, Goal Identification Form. Once you have agreed upon specific actions the sport director will take to assist in achieving each goal, write those actions in the spaces below.

First goal

Action 1: _____

Action 2: _____

Second goal

Action 1: _____

Action 2: _____

Third goal

Action 1: _____

Action 2: _____

Step 4: Identify criteria for determining goal achievement.

For each of the goals listed in Step 1, list two criteria by which the individual and the sport director will determine whether the goal has been met.

First goal

Criteria 1: _____

Criteria 2: _____

Second goal

Criteria 1: _____

Criteria 2: _____

Third goal

Criteria 1: _____

Criteria 2: _____

Use the space below to include any additional comments relating to the goal-setting conference.

 **Form 2.8**

PROGRESS APPRAISAL CONFERENCE FORM

Sport directors and personnel should use this form to facilitate an appraisal of the progress made toward the goals presented in Form 2.7, Goal-Setting Conference Form. Although the sport director should take responsibility for filling in the items on this form, the sport director and the individual being evaluated should work together to determine the best responses for each step. Remember that the formative evaluation process is designed to assist personnel in achieving their own goals for professional growth and development. This form is designed to help the sport director and that individual review the actions taken to achieve those goals.

Name: _____   Position: _____

Sport director: _____   Date: _____

Step 1: Review actions taken to achieve goals.

Examine the goals identified in Step 1 of Form 2.7, Goal-Setting Conference Form. For each goal, describe the specific actions the individual took to reach his or her goal.

First goal

Specific actions taken: _____

_____

_____

Second goal

Specific actions taken: _____

_____

_____

Third goal

Specific actions taken: _____

_____

_____

Step 2: Review actions sport director has taken to assist pursuit of goals.

Describe the specific actions the sport director took to assist in achieving these goals.

First goal

Specific actions taken: _____

_____

_____

Second goal

Specific actions taken: _____

_____

_____

Third goal

Specific actions taken: _____

_____

_____

Step 3: Review criteria and determine progress made toward achieving goals.

Refer to Step 4 of Form 2.7, Goal-Setting Conference Form, and examine the criteria by which the individual and the sport director decided they would determine whether the goal had been met. Circle the appropriate response below to indicate whether the goal has been met. Then, use the space labeled "Comments" to explain why the goal either was or was not met, as well as any additional information relating to the individual's professional development.

First goal

Was this goal met?   yes   no

Comments: _____

_____

_____

Second goal

Was this goal met?   yes   no

Comments: _____

_____

_____

Third goal

Was this goal met?   yes   no

Comments: _____

_____

_____

Step 4: Reflect on the process and make notes for future professional growth.

Use the space below to note additional information regarding this year's formative evaluation process and to make suggestions for next year's goal-setting process.

_____   _____

Signature of individual being evaluated   Date

_____   _____

Signature of sport director   Date

Form 2.9

PERSONNEL EVALUATION SUMMARY FORM

This form is designed to assist you in assembling the results from the other forms for each of your personnel. As you complete this form, you will review the results of the other forms and obtain a summary of your staff's strengths and weaknesses which you can use in enhancing your program next year.

Name: _____

I. Summative coach evaluation

If the individual whose name appears above is not a coach, skip to section VI. First, enter the dates this year that you or a designated supervisor observed the individual whose name appears above. Next, review the results of Form 2.1, Summative Coach Evaluation Instrument, which were completed during those observations. Use the spaces below to list any concerns you have regarding the individual's approach to athletes' safety, duty proficiency, and administrative competence. Finally, write a brief statement to summarize your recommendations for this individual's continued employment.

Observation dates: _____ _____ _____ _____

Concerns:

_____

_____

_____

Recommendations:

_____

_____

_____

II. Colleague questionnaires

Now, enter the general information on the lines below to indicate the dates that Form 2.2, Colleague Questionnaire, was distributed and collected, as well as the number of forms that were sent out and collected. Next, look over the results of these forms (see suggestions for analyzing results on pages 26–29 of the guide), and list your primary concerns in the space provided.

Date sent: _____   Number sent: _____

Date collected: _____   Number collected: _____

Concerns:

_____

_____

_____

III. Athlete questionnaires

Repeat the procedure you just followed in section II. This time, however, report the results for Form 2.3, Athlete Questionnaire.

Date sent: _____   Number sent: _____

Date collected: _____   Number collected: _____

Concerns:

_____

_____

_____

IV. Parent questionnaires

Once again, repeat the procedure you followed in sections II and III, this time reporting the results for Form 2.4, Parent Questionnaire.

Date sent: _____   Number sent: _____

Date collected: _____   Number collected: _____

Concerns:

_____

_____

_____

V. Coach self-appraisal

Now write the date on the line below to indicate when you received Form 2.5, Coach Self-Appraisal Form. Look over the results of that form and make comments about how the coach's self-appraisal compared to the results obtained using Forms 2.2, Colleague Questionnaire; 2.3, Athlete Questionnaire; and 2.4, Parent Questionnaire.

Date collected: _____

Comments:

_____

_____

_____

VI. Formative evaluation

Use the spaces below to report the results of your formative evaluation process. First, write in the dates when the goal-setting and progress appraisal conferences were held. Next, copy the goals from Step 1 of Form 2.7, Goal-Setting Conference Form, into the space labeled "Goals." Finally, briefly summarize your appraisal of the individual being evaluated and note important considerations for next year's evaluation process.

Goal-setting conference date: _____

Progress appraisal conference date: _____

Goals:

1. _____

2. _____

3. _____

Comments:

_____

_____

_____

_____

_____

_____

 **Form 3.1**

FACILITIES INSPECTION CHECKLIST

Name of inspector _____

Date of inspection _____

Name and location of facility _____

_____

Note: Form 3.1 is an incomplete checklist provided as an example. Use it to develop a checklist specific for your facilities.

Facility Condition

Circle Y (yes) if the facility is in good condition and N (no) if it needs something done to make it acceptable. In the space provided note what needs to be done.

Gymnasium

Y   N   Floor (no water spots, buckling, loose sections) _____

Y   N   Walls (vandalism free) _____

Y   N   Lights (all functioning) _____

Y   N   Windows (secure) _____

Y   N   Roof (no adverse impact of weather) _____

Y   N   Stairs (well lighted)_____

Y   N   Bleachers (support structure sound) _____

Y   N   Exits (lights working) _____

Y   N   Basketball rims (level, securely attached) _____

Y   N   Basketball backboards (no cracks, clean) _____

Y   N   Mats (clean, properly stored, no defects) _____

Y   N   Uprights/projections _____

Y   N   Wall plugs (covered) _____

Y   N   Light switches (all functioning) _____

Y   N   Heating/cooling system (temperature control) _____

Y   N   Ducts, radiators, pipes _____

Y   N   Thermostats _____

Y   N   Fire alarms (regularly checked) _____

Y   N   Directions posted for evacuating the gym in case of fire _____

Y   N   Fire extinguishers (regularly checked) _____

Other (list) _____

_____

Locker room(s)

Y   N   Floor _____

Y   N   Walls _____

Y   N   Lights _____

Y   N   Windows _____

Y   N   Roof _____

Y   N   Showers _____

Y   N   Drains _____

Y   N   Benches _____

Y   N   Lockers _____

Y   N   Exits _____

Y   N   Water fountains _____

Y   N   Toilets _____

Y   N   Trainer's room _____

Other (list) _____

_____

Field(s)/outside playing area

Surface

Y   N   Not too wet or too dry _____

Y   N   Grass length _____

Y   N   Free of debris _____

Y   N   Free of holes and bumps _____

Y   N   Free of protruding pipes, wires, lines _____

Y   N   Line markers _____

Stands

Y   N   Pitching mound _____

Y   N   Dugouts _____

Y   N   Warning track and fences _____

Y   N   Sidelines _____

Y   N   Sprinklers _____

Y   N   Garbage _____

Y   N   Security fences _____

Y   N   Water fountains _____

Y   N   Storage sheds _____

Concession Area

Y   N   Electrical_____

Y   N   Heating/cooling systems_____

Other (list) _____

_____

Pool

Y   N   Equipment in good repair _____

Y   N   Sanitary_____

Y   N   Slipperiness on decks and diving board controlled _____

Y   N   Chemicals safely stored _____

Y   N   Regulations and safety rules posted _____

Lighting—adequate visibility

Y   N   No glare _____

Y   N   Penetrates to bottom of pool_____

Y   N   Exit light in good repair _____

Y   N   Halls and locker rooms meet code requirements _____

Y   N   Light switches properly grounded _____

Y   N   Has emergency generator to back up regular power source _____

Exits—accessible, secure

Y   N   Adequate size, number _____

Y   N   Self-closing doors_____

Y   N   Self-locking doors _____

Y   N   Striker plates secure _____

Y   N   No obstacles or debris _____

Y   N   Office and storage rooms locked _____

Ring buoys

Y   N   20-inch diameter_____

Y   N   50-foot rope length _____

Reaching poles

Y   N   One each side _____

Y   N   12-foot length _____

Y   N   Metal stress_____

Y   N   Good repair _____

Guard chair(s)

    Y   N   Unobstructed view _____

    Y   N   Tall enough to see bottom of pool _____

Safety line at break point in the pool grade (deep end)

    Y   N   Bright color floats_____

    Y   N   3/4-inch rope_____

First aid kit

    Y   N   Inventoried and replenished regularly _____

Stretcher, two blankets, and spine board

    Y   N   Inventoried and in good repair _____

Emergency telephone, lights, and public address system

    Y   N   Accessible_____

    Y   N   Directions for use posted visibly _____

    Y   N   Powered by emergency generators as well as regular power system _____

    Y   N   Emergency numbers on telephone cradle or receiver_____

Emergency procedures

    Y   N   Sign posted in highly visible area_____

Track

Surface

    Y   N   Free of debris _____

    Y   N   Free of holes and bumps_____

    Y   N   Throwing circles_____

    Y   N   Fences _____

    Y   N   Water fountains_____

Other (list) _____

_____

Recommendations/observations: _____

_____

_____

_____

_____

_____

_____

 **Form 3.2**

EQUIPMENT INSPECTION CHECKLIST

Name of inspector _____

Date of inspection _____

> *Note:* Form 3.2 is an incomplete checklist provided as an example. Use it to develop a checklist specific for your equipment.

Equipment Condition

Circle Y (yes) if the equipment is in good condition and N (no) if it needs something done to make it acceptable. In the space provided note what needs to be done.

Football

Y   N   Helmets _____

Y   N   Mouth guards _____

Y   N   Jerseys _____

Y   N   Pants _____

Y   N   Shoulder pads _____

Y   N   Hip pads/girdle _____

Y   N   Thigh pads _____

Y   N   Elbow pads _____

Y   N   Hand pads _____

Y   N   Shoes/spikes _____

Y   N   Footballs _____

Other (list)

_____

_____

Basketball

Y   N   Jerseys _____

Y   N   Shorts _____

Y   N   Shoes _____

Y   N   Mouth guards (optional) _____

Y   N   Eye guards/goggles (optional) _____

Y   N   Knee pads _____

Y   N   Elbow pads _____

Y   N   Basketballs _____

Other (list)

_____

_____

Wrestling

Y   N   Singlets _____

Y   N   Shoes _____

Y   N   Headgear _____

Other (list)

_____

_____

Baseball

Y   N   Jerseys _____

Y   N   Pants _____

Y   N   Sliding pants/pads _____

Y   N   Leggings _____

Y   N   Protective cups _____

Y   N   Mouth guards (optional) _____

Y   N   Eye guards/goggles (optional) _____

Y   N   Caps _____

Y   N   Cleats/shoes _____

Y   N   Baseballs _____

Y   N   Bats _____

Y   N   Batting gloves _____

Y   N   Bases _____

Y   N   Gloves _____

Other (list)

_____

_____

Softball

Y   N   Jerseys _____

Y   N   Pants/shorts _____

Y   N   Leggings _____

Y   N   Sliding pants/pads _____

Y   N   Protective cups _____

Y   N   Mouth guards (optional) _____

Y   N   Eye guards/goggles (optional) _____

Y   N   Caps _____

Y   N   Cleats/shoes _____

Y   N   Softballs _____

Y   N   Bats _____

Y   N   Batting gloves _____

Y   N   Bases _____

Y   N   Gloves _____

Other (list)

_____

_____

Tennis

Y   N   Shirts/jerseys _____

Y   N   Shorts _____

Y   N   Shoes _____

Y   N   Mouth guards (optional) _____

Y   N   Eye guards/goggles (optional) _____

Y   N   Racquets _____

Y   N   Tennis balls _____

Other (list)

_____

_____

Volleyball

Y   N   Shirts/jerseys _____

Y   N   Shorts _____

Y   N   Shoes _____

Y   N   Mouth guards (optional) _____

Y   N   Eye guards/goggles (optional) _____

Y   N   Knee pads _____

Y   N   Elbow pads _____

Y   N   Volleyballs _____

Other (list)

_____

_____

Soccer

Y N Jerseys _____

Y N Shorts _____

Y N Shoes _____

Y N Mouth guards (optional) _____

Y N Eye guards/goggles (optional) _____

Y N Shin guards _____

Y N Soccer balls _____

Other (list)

_____

_____

Hockey

Y N Helmets/chin straps _____

Y N Mouth guards _____

Y N Jerseys _____

Y N Pants _____

Y N Protective cups/supporters _____

Y N Ankle guards _____

Y N Shoulder pads _____

Y N Suspenders/belts/garters _____

Y N Sticks _____

Y N Shin pads _____

Y N Thigh pads _____

Y N Elbow pads _____

Y N Gloves _____

Y N Socks _____

Y N Shorts/long underwear _____

Y N Skates _____

Y N Pucks _____

Other (list)

_____

_____

 **Form 3.3**

RECORD-KEEPING CHECKLIST

Use this form to track the status of important facility and equipment records for your program. Use one copy of this form for each of your program offerings. Use a single file folder to store a copy of this form for each of your program offerings and check the folder regularly to determine which records may require follow up.

I. Program identification

Use the first line to describe the program offering covered by this form (i.e., girls' track and field). On the second line, list the name of the head coach for the program, and on the next lines list the names of any assistant coaches and athletic trainers.

Sport/program: _____

Coach: _____

Assistant: _____

Trainer: _____

II. Record log

Fill in the "Date due" column to indicate when each of the records listed in this section should be returned to the athletic program office. As these records are submitted, use the "Date received" column to indicate the date you received each record, and use the "Location and comments" column to indicate where each record has been filed and any other comments to remind you of the need to follow up.

Record	Date due	Date received	Location and comments
Status reports			
Inventory	_____	_____	_____
Facility checklist	_____	_____	_____
Equipment checklist	_____	_____	_____
Maintenance records			
Facility repairs	_____	_____	_____
Facility care	_____	_____	_____
Equipment repairs	_____	_____	_____
Equipment care	_____	_____	_____
Planning records			
Facility schedule	_____	_____	_____
Budget	_____	_____	_____
Equipment requests	_____	_____	_____
Other records			
_____	_____	_____	_____
_____	_____	_____	_____
_____	_____	_____	_____

Form 3.4

FACILITY ANALYSIS FORM

Use this form to analyze each of your program's facilities. Make a separate copy of the form for each facility.

Date: _____

I. Description

Use the first line below to identify the facility analyzed on this form. Then, list as many uses of that facility as you can. Include as many sport program and other uses (i.e., concerts, art shows, etc.) as possible to provide you with a complete picture of the many ways the facility is used.

Facility: _____

Uses:

_____

_____

_____

_____

_____

_____

II. Accommodations

First, indicate the capacity of this facility for athletes or teams and spectators. Next, circle "yes" or "no" to indicate whether concessions, restrooms, lockers, storage, media, and other facilities are available. Then use the "comments" line to note any important information about each of these accommodations that will help you record an accurate picture of the features of the facility.

Capacity: Athletes/teams _____   Spectators _____

Concessions: yes   no   comments: _____

Restrooms: yes   no   comments: _____

Lockers: yes   no   comments: _____

Storage: yes   no   comments: _____

Media: yes   no   comments: _____

Other: yes   no   comments: _____

Other: yes   no   comments: _____

III. Expenses

Now you are ready to list the expenses incurred to operate the facility. Use the spaces below to detail the monthly and annual cost of rent, utilities, maintenance, and operation of the facility. Be sure to use the last lines to total monthly and annual expenses for the facility.

Rent: $_____ monthly $_____ annually

Utilities: $_____ monthly $_____ annually

Maintenance: $_____ monthly $_____ annually

Operation: $_____ monthly $_____ annually

Other: $_____ monthly $_____ annually

Totals: $_____ monthly $_____ annually

IV. Schedule of use

Finally, fill in the boxes below each month with the names and dates when sports, programs, and special events rely on this facility. When you have completed this section of the form, you will have a pretty good view of when your facility is in greatest demand, as well as times when you may be able to make better use of the facility. Use the "Comments" section at the end of this form to note any additional questions, comments, or concerns about this facility.

Aug	Sep	Oct	Nov	Dec	Jan

Feb	Mar	Apr	May	Jun	Jul

Comments:

 **Form 3.5**

EQUIPMENT ANALYSIS FORM

Use this form to analyze the equipment for each of your program offerings. Make a separate copy of the form for each program. Use the top line of the form to identify the program analyzed on this form. When you have completed the form, you should have listed all equipment and uniforms used by the program.

Date: _____

Sport/program: _____

Equipment status

I. Items in good condition

On the lines beneath "Description/date purchased," first list all equipment that is currently in good condition (meaning it will likely be usable not only this season, but next season as well). Next to each description, write the date that item was initially purchased. Finally, use the "Quantity" column to indicate the number of each item currently in good condition. Each item should appear on a separate line. For example, if you have 36 practice jerseys, 17 white and 19 gold, you would list the white jerseys on one line and the gold jerseys on the next line.

Description/date purchased   Quantity

_____   _____

_____   _____

_____   _____

_____   _____

_____   _____

_____   _____

_____   _____

_____   _____

_____   _____

_____   _____

_____   _____

_____   _____

_____   _____

_____   _____

_____   _____

_____   _____

II. Items in poor condition

Begin by listing in the first column the description and date of purchase for all items in poor condition. Any equipment not listed in section I (in good condition) should appear here. Next, use the "Quantity" column to indicate the number of each item currently in poor condition. Check catalogs or call vendors to obtain information on the cost to repair and replace each item and enter the results in the "Repair cost" and "Replace cost" columns. Use the last column to enter your recommendation for repairing or replacing each item, along with the cost for following your recommendation. Finally, add the costs you have listed in the last column and enter the total in the "Total cost" box at the bottom of the list.

Description/date purchased	Quantity	Repair cost	Replace cost	Recommendation/cost
			Total cost:	

III. New items to purchase

Begin by listing in the first column the description of any new equipment that should be purchased. Next, use the "Quantity" column to indicate the number of each item that should be purchased. Check catalogs or call vendors to obtain information on the cost of each item and enter the results in the "Cost" column. Finally, add the costs you have listed in the last column and enter the total in the "Total cost" box at the bottom of the list. Use the "Comments" section at the end of this form to note any additional questions, comments, or concerns about equipment for this program.

Description	Quantity	Cost
	Total cost:	

Comments:

 **Form 3.6**

FACILITIES AND EQUIPMENT QUESTIONNAIRE

Sport/program: _____   Date distributed: _____

Please return to: _____   **Please return by:** _____

We are requesting that you take a few moments to provide feedback about your program's facilities and equipment. To complete the form, circle the response that best describes your opinion for each item. If the answer is difficult to determine, or cannot be determined at this time, circle the question mark. In the space below each descriptor, labeled "Comments," write a brief explanation of what led you to circle your response. Thank you in advance for your time.

1. Practice facilities are in good physical condition.	yes	no	?
Comments:			
2. Contest facilities are in good physical condition.	yes	no	?
Comments:			
3. Locker facilities are conveniently located for practices and contests.	yes	no	?
Comments:			
4. There are sufficient locker facilities for my athletes.	yes	no	?
Comments:			
5. Facilities are maintained appropriately.	yes	no	?
Comments:			
6. Facilities have adequate ventilation.	yes	no	?
Comments:			
7. Facility temperatures are moderated appropriately.	yes	no	?
Comments:			

8. Facilities have adequate lighting.	yes	no	?
Comments:			

9. Storage facilities are conveniently located.	yes	no	?
Comments:			

10. Storage facilities are adequate for my equipment.	yes	no	?
Comments:			

11. Rented facilities meet the needs of my program.	yes	no	?
Comments:			

12. Strength and conditioning facilities are appropriately equipped.	yes	no	?
Comments:			

13. I have access to equipment necessary to ensure the safety of my athletes.	yes	no	?
Comments:			

14. Equipment is repaired and replaced appropriately.	yes	no	?
Comments:			

15. Rented equipment meets the needs of my program.	yes	no	?
Comments:			

16. Uniforms are replaced at appropriate intervals.	yes	no	?
Comments:			

Please use the space below for additional comments regarding the adequacy of facilities and equipment for your program.

Thank you for your time!

 **Form 3.7**

FACILITY AND EQUIPMENT EVALUATION SUMMARY FORM

Use this form to summarize the results of your facility and equipment evaluation. Use the first page to summarize facilities and the second page to summarize equipment. Make enough copies of each page to cover all of your programs and their facilities.

Date: _____

I. Facility summary

Complete a separate box for each of your facilities. First use the "Facility description" box to write a brief description of the facility. Next, use the box under "Recommendations" to briefly list your recommendations for that facility, including repairs and modifications that need to be made. Finally, use the box under "Cost" to list the costs of the recommendations you have made for that facility.

Facility description:	
Recommendations	Cost

Facility description:	
Recommendations	Cost

Facility description:	
Recommendations	Cost

II. Equipment summary

Complete a separate box for each piece of equipment in need of repair or replacement. First use the "Equipment description" box to write a brief description of the equipment. Next, use the box under "Recommendations" to briefly list your recommendations for repairing or replacing that equipment. Finally, use the box under "Cost" to list the costs of the recommendations you have made for that equipment.

Equipment description:	
Recommendations	Cost

Equipment description:	
Recommendations	Cost

Equipment description:	
Recommendations	Cost

Equipment description:	
Recommendations	Cost

 **Form 3.8**

SPORT DIRECTOR'S PROGRAM IDENTIFICATION FORM

Use this form to create a complete list of all your program offerings, as well as to indicate the number of participants in each offering.

I. Interscholastic sports

For each interscholastic sport program offered by your organization, circle the gender descriptors to indicate whether programs exist only for males, only for females, for both males and females (circle both "male" and "female"), or as coed programs. Next, indicate the number of individuals who participated in these programs last year and this year. You may keep track of male and female participation by entering those numbers separately for "last year" and "this year." Either use a slash [/] or space to keep these numbers separate. For example, if your cross-country program included 15 males and 23 females last year, simply enter 15/23 on the line indicating "Number of participants" last year.

Sport	*Gender (circle)*			*Number of participants*	
1. baseball	male	female	coed	_____ last year	_____ this year
2. basketball	male	female	coed	_____ last year	_____ this year
3. cheerleading	male	female	coed	_____ last year	_____ this year
4. cross-country	male	female	coed	_____ last year	_____ this year
5. diving	male	female	coed	_____ last year	_____ this year
6. football	male	female	coed	_____ last year	_____ this year
7. golf	male	female	coed	_____ last year	_____ this year
8. gymnastics	male	female	coed	_____ last year	_____ this year
9. field hockey	male	female	coed	_____ last year	_____ this year
10. ice hockey	male	female	coed	_____ last year	_____ this year
11. in-line hockey	male	female	coed	_____ last year	_____ this year
12. lacrosse	male	female	coed	_____ last year	_____ this year
13. skiing	male	female	coed	_____ last year	_____ this year
14. soccer	male	female	coed	_____ last year	_____ this year
15. softball	male	female	coed	_____ last year	_____ this year
16. swimming	male	female	coed	_____ last year	_____ this year
17. tennis	male	female	coed	_____ last year	_____ this year
18. track and field	male	female	coed	_____ last year	_____ this year
19. volleyball	male	female	coed	_____ last year	_____ this year
20. wrestling	male	female	coed	_____ last year	_____ this year
21. _____	male	female	coed	_____ last year	_____ this year
22. _____	male	female	coed	_____ last year	_____ this year

II. Club sports

Use the first column to list each club sport program offered by your organization. Then complete this section by following the instructions given for the first section of the form.

Sport	Gender (circle)			Number of participants	
1. _____	male	female	coed	_____ last year	_____ this year
2. _____	male	female	coed	_____ last year	_____ this year
3. _____	male	female	coed	_____ last year	_____ this year
4. _____	male	female	coed	_____ last year	_____ this year
5. _____	male	female	coed	_____ last year	_____ this year
6. _____	male	female	coed	_____ last year	_____ this year
7. _____	male	female	coed	_____ last year	_____ this year
8. _____	male	female	coed	_____ last year	_____ this year
9. _____	male	female	coed	_____ last year	_____ this year
10. _____	male	female	coed	_____ last year	_____ this year

III. Intramural sports

Use the first column to list each intramural sport program offered by your organization. Then complete this section by following the instructions given for the first section of the form.

Sport	Gender (circle)			Number of participants	
1. _____	male	female	coed	_____ last year	_____ this year
2. _____	male	female	coed	_____ last year	_____ this year
3. _____	male	female	coed	_____ last year	_____ this year
4. _____	male	female	coed	_____ last year	_____ this year
5. _____	male	female	coed	_____ last year	_____ this year
6. _____	male	female	coed	_____ last year	_____ this year
7. _____	male	female	coed	_____ last year	_____ this year
8. _____	male	female	coed	_____ last year	_____ this year
9. _____	male	female	coed	_____ last year	_____ this year
10. _____	male	female	coed	_____ last year	_____ this year

IV. Other programs

Use the first column to list any other athletic programs offered by your organization. Then complete this section by following the instructions given for the first section of the form.

	Sport	*Gender (circle)*			*Number of participants*	
1.	_____	male	female	coed	_____ last year	_____ this year
2.	_____	male	female	coed	_____ last year	_____ this year
3.	_____	male	female	coed	_____ last year	_____ this year
4.	_____	male	female	coed	_____ last year	_____ this year
5.	_____	male	female	coed	_____ last year	_____ this year
6.	_____	male	female	coed	_____ last year	_____ this year
7.	_____	male	female	coed	_____ last year	_____ this year
8.	_____	male	female	coed	_____ last year	_____ this year
9.	_____	male	female	coed	_____ last year	_____ this year
10.	_____	male	female	cocd	_____ last year	_____ this year

 **Form 3.9**

SPORT PROGRAM QUESTIONNAIRE

Date distributed: _____

Please return to: _____   **Please return by:** _____

Because we feel it is essential to monitor the breadth and depth of our sport programs we are requesting that you take a few moments to provide feedback about our program offerings. Your responses will be kept confidential.

To complete the form, circle the response that best describes your opinion for each item. If the answer is difficult to determine, or cannot be determined at this time, circle the question mark. In the space below each descriptor, labeled "Comments," write a brief explanation of what led you to circle your response. Thank you in advance for your time.

1. Our sport programs offer a good variety of choices for athletes.	yes	no	?
Comments:			
2. Our sport programs provide opportunities for athletes of varying socioeconomic status.	yes	no	?
Comments:			
3. Our sport programs provide equal opportunities for male and female athletes.	yes	no	?
Comments:			
4. Our sport programs provide equal opportunities for individuals with disabilities.	yes	no	?
Comments:			
5. Our sport programs provide equal opportunities for individuals of varying race and ethnicity.	yes	no	?
Comments:			

6. Our sport programs provide opportunities for individuals interested in pursuing athletics at a higher level.	yes	no	?
Comments:			
7. Our sport programs provide opportunities for athletes interested only in fitness and enjoyment.	yes	no	?
Comments:			
8. Our sport program offerings are safe for athletes.	yes	no	?
Comments:			
9. Our sport programs encourage life-long fitness and health.	yes	no	?
Comments:			
10. Our sport programs emphasize development of athletes over winning.	yes	no	?
Comments:			
11. Our sport programs are a valuable part of athletes' educational experiences.	yes	no	?
Comments:			
12. Are there any sports you would like us to consider adding?	yes	no	?
Comments:			
13. Are there any sports you would like us to consider discontinuing?	yes	no	?
Comments:			

Please use the space below to provide additional feedback regarding the quality, depth, and breadth of our sport programs.

Thank you for your time!

 **Form 3.10**

PROGRAM ANALYSIS SUMMARY FORM

Use this form to summarize the results of your program offering evaluation.

I. Program questionnaires analysis

Enter the general information on the lines below to indicate the dates that Form 3.9, Sport Program Questionnaire, was distributed and collected, as well as the number of these forms that were sent out and collected. Next, look over results of these forms (see suggestions for analyzing results on pages 26–29 of the guide), and list your quality and safety concerns in the space provided. Now proceed by listing your concerns over the depth and breadth of program offerings under "Depth and breadth concerns." Conclude this section of the form by completing the "Access concerns" in the space provided.

Date sent: _____   Number sent: _____

Date collected: _____   Number collected: _____

Quality and safety concerns:

_____

_____

_____

_____

_____

Depth and breadth concerns:

_____

_____

_____

_____

Access concerns:

_____

_____

_____

_____

II. Program cost analysis

Use this part of the form to summarize the costs of operating your sport program. Note that the next page is a blank form that you may copy as many times as necessary to allow you to enter information for all of your sport program offerings. Begin by entering the name of a sport program in the first box under "Sport." Next, enter expenses for that sport under the categories listed. Spaces have been provided for you to enter expenses for salaries, facilities, equipment, and transportation. In addition, use the "Other" column for expenses not covered by one of these categories. Now proceed by entering the income generated by the sport. Use the "Fees" column to enter income from participation or other fees, and the "Receipts" column to enter income such as that generated by admissions. Add together the "Fees" and "Receipts" columns, then subtract the amounts listed under the various categories of "Expenses" to arrive at the number you will enter in the last column, "Net expense/income." If the result is a negative number, which will often be the case, either use a minus sign before the number or, in accordance with standard bookkeeping procedures, place the number in parentheses.

Sport	Expenses					Income		Net expense/ income
	Salary	Facility	Equipment	Transport	Other	Fees	Receipts	

Sport	Expenses					Income		Net expense/ income
	Salary	Facility	Equipment	Transport	Other	Fees	Receipts	

III. Concerns and recommendations

After reviewing the results of the previous sections, use the following spaces to record concerns and recommendations for your athletic program offerings.

Concerns:

_____

_____

_____

_____

_____

_____

_____

_____

Recommendations:

_____

_____

_____

_____

_____

_____

_____

Appendix

American Sport Education Program (ASEP) Leader Level Resources

Item	Item number	Unit price*
Leader Level Coaching Principles Course Materials		
Leader Level Coaching Principles Course (*Successful Coaching*, *Clinic Study Guide*, Course Processing, Diploma)	ACEP0080	30.00
Successful Coaching	PMAR0376	18.00
Coaching Principles Instructor Guide (Rev. 3rd Ed.)	ACEP0007	70.00
Coaching Principles Clinic Study Guide (package of 10)	ACEP0033	22.50
Coaching Principles Leadership Training Seminar	ACEP0056	299.00
Leader Level Coaching Principles Videotape Set (5)	MACE0100	325.00
Coaching Philosophy Videotape	MACE0101	70.00
Sport Psychology Videotape	MACE0102	70.00
Sport Pedagogy Videotape	MACE0103	70.00
Sport Physiology Videotape	MACE0104	70.00
Sport Management Videotape	MACE0105	70.00
NFICEP Coaching Principles Course Materials		
NFICEP Coaching Principles Course (*Successful Coaching*, *Clinic Study Guide*, Course Processing, Diploma)	ACEP0083	30.00
Successful Coaching (NFICEP Edition)	ACEP0064	18.00
Coaching Principles Instructor Guide	ACEP0005	70.00
Coaching Principles Leadership Training Seminar	ACEP0058	299.00

Item	Item number	Unit price*
NFICEP Coaching Principles Videotape Set (5)	MNFI0100	325.00
Coaching Philosophy Videotape	MNFI0101	70.00
Sport Psychology Videotape	MNFI0102	70.00
Sport Pedagogy Videotape	MNFI0103	70.00
Sport Physiology Videotape	MNFI0104	70.00
Sport Management Videotape	MNFI0105	70.00

Leader Level Sport First Aid Course Materials

Item	Item number	Unit price*
Leader Level Sport First Aid Course (*Sport First Aid*, *Clinic Study Guide*, Course Processing, Diploma)	ACEP0081	30.00
Sport First Aid	PFLE0410	18.00
Sport First Aid Instructor Guide	ACEP0004	70.00
Sport First Aid Clinic Study Guide (package of 10)	ACEP0036	22.50
Sport First Aid Leadership Training Seminar	ACEP0068	199.00
Leader Level Sport First Aid Videotape	MACE0106	125.00

NFICEP Sport First Aid Course Materials

Item	Item number	Unit price*
NFICEP Sport First Aid Course (*Sport First Aid*, *Clinic Study Guide*, Course Processing, Diploma)	ACEP0082	30.00
Sport First Aid (NFICEP Edition)	ACEP0065	18.00
Sport First Aid Instructor Guide	ACEP0006	70.00
Sport First Aid Leadership Training Seminar	ACEP0070	199.00
Leader Level Sport First Aid Videotape	MNFI0106	125.00

Leader Level/NFICEP Drugs and Sport Course Materials

Item	Item number	Unit price*
Coaches Guide to Drugs and Sport	PRIN0715	17.95

Leader Level Sport Techniques and Tactics Resources

Item	Item number	Unit price*
Coaching Basketball Successfully	PWOO0446	18.95
Coaching Girls' Basketball Successfully	PHUT0343	20.00
Coaching Football Successfully	PREA0518	18.95
Coaching Swimming Successfully	PHAN0492	18.95
Coaching Tennis Successfully	PUST0461	18.95
Coaching Volleyball Successfully	PNEV0362	18.00

Leader Level SportDirector Resources

Item	Item number	Unit price*
Event Management for SportDirectors	ACEP0320	20.00
Program Evaluation for SportDirectors	PKES0505	20.00
Promotion for SportDirectors	PJOH0722	20.00

*ALL PRICES ARE SUBJECT TO CHANGE. Call ASEP at (800) 747-5698 for current price information.

About the Author

James Kestner is Development Director for the American Sport Education Program, where he develops educational programs and books, videos, and software resources for coaches, sport administrators, and parents. After completing his undergraduate education at Eastern Illinois University in Charleston, Jim taught English at Woodland High School in Streator, Illinois. Later, he taught English and coached cross-country and track and field at Oakland High School in Oakland, Illinois.

In 1993 Jim received a master's degree in educational administration with a concentration in staff development from the University of Illinois at Urbana-Champaign (UIUC). While working toward his degree, Jim served as a consultant for teacher evaluation instruments, wrote grants, and served as a consultant for the National Center for School Leadership.

Currently a doctoral student at UIUC, Jim is working toward a PhD in educational administration with a concentration in school finance and program evaluation. His accomplishments at UIUC include publishing articles on new teacher induction and school finance, evaluating reading improvement programs and Illinois state school consolidation initiatives, and serving on a number of Illinois School Improvement committees. In addition, he has earned recognition for his outstanding achievement in education through the Linda S. Lotto Scholarship and through the College of Education as a William Chandler Bagley Scholar. Jim is a member of the UIUC Educational Administration Alumni Association and the American Society for Public Administration. His hobbies include running; fishing; basketball; and writing articles, short stories, and poetry.

American Sport Education Program

Leader Level

ASEP's Leader Level provides quality resources and courses for coaches and administrators in interscholastic and club sport. In fact, the National Federation of State High School Associations has selected the Leader Level SportCoach Courses as its own coaches education program, called NFICEP–National Federation Interscholastic Coaches Education Program. The Leader Level offers the following:

Leadership Training Seminars

Our Leadership Training Seminars (LTSs) not only show sport administrators how to conduct our courses, they also revitalize them with fresh ideas about how to help coaches be more effective in their coaching roles. Leader Level instructor seminars include the

- Coaching Principles Seminar,
- Sport First Aid Seminar, and
- Drugs and Sport Seminar (in development).

Coaches Courses

Once administrators have attended our LTSs, they are prepared to teach our **Coaching Principles Course** and **Sport First Aid Course,** and soon, the **Drugs and Sport Course** to coaches. The courses provide excellent educational opportunities for both new and experienced coaches. At each course, coaches attend a clinic, study the course text and study guide, then take an open-book test.

The Coaching Successfully Series

The books in this series explain how to teach fundamental sports skills and strategies as well as how to build a sports program by applying principles of philosophy, psychology, and teaching and management methods to coaching.

Series Titles
- Coaching Tennis Successfully
- Coaching Swimming Successfully
- Coaching Football Successfully
- Coaching Basketball Successfully
- Coaching Volleyball Successfully
- Coaching Girls' Basketball Successfully
- Coaching Baseball Successfully

SportDirector Series

See facing page for information.

For more information about ASEP and the Leader Level, call toll-free 1-800-747-5698.

Other Resources in the SportDirector Series

Event Management for SportDirectors
American Sport Education Program

1996 • Spiral • 144 pp • Item ACEP0320
ISBN 0-87322-968-1 • $20.00 ($29.95 Canadian)

Event Management for SportDirectors is a handy tool for planning and managing practically any type or size of athletic event. The book provides a comprehensive checklist of 18 categories (with tasks to be completed for each category), allowing you to conduct even the most complicated functions in a systematic and organized manner.

This time-saving resource shows you how to plan and manage the following areas of an event:

- Event objectives
- Finances
- Rules and officials
- Coach development
- Risk management
- Registration
- Communications
- Event evaluation
- Awards
- Food service
- Transportation
- Housing
- Promotion
- Public relations
- Facility needs
- Staffing
- Practice and competition schedules
- Equipment, uniforms, and supplies

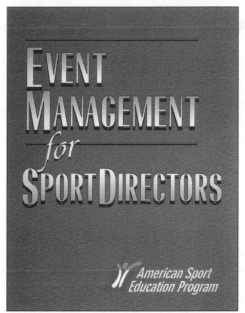

Promotion for SportDirectors
John R. Johnson

1996 • Paper • Approx 144 pp • Item PJOH0722
ISBN 0-87322-722-0 • $20.00 ($29.95 Canadian)

This one-of-a-kind resource will help you properly promote your high school's athletic program and give it the visibility it deserves! The book not only reviews all the promotional tools that are at your disposal, but also explains how to make them an integral part of your program's daily operations.

First, you'll learn how to plan for an effective promotion program. You'll discover how your school's philosophy about promotion meshes with your own, how to assess your promotion needs and limitations, and how to develop a comprehensive promotional plan.

You'll also learn how to implement a positive public relations program, develop and distribute printed promotions such as programs and schedules, take advantage of radio and television promotion, boost attendance using special promotions, and obtain program sponsorships.

2335